T0354914

WHO IS RIGHT?

Zimi Roberto

Order this book online at www.trafford.com
or email orders@trafford.com

Most Trafford titles are also available at major online book retailers.

Print information available on the last page.

ISBN: 978-1-4120-9521-1 (sc)

Trafford rev. 07/09/2019

North America & international
toll-free: 1 888 232 4444 (USA & Canada)
fax: 812 355 4082

CONTENTS

Acknowledgements i
Introduction iii
WHO IS RIGHT? xi

CHAPTER ONE 1
Has Blair Retreated from his "Regime Change" in Zimbabwe? 3

CHAPTER TWO 49
Why Are British MPs Furious at Presidents Mugabe and Mbeki? 51

CHAPTER THREE 85
Lack of Honourable Interest in Africa Within the House of
Commons – A Research Work 87

CHAPTER FOUR 97
My Criticism of Disingenuous British Parliamentarians/Politicians 99

CONCLUSION 129
Overall Conclusion 131

APPENDIX 1: 143
The bitterness and long-lasting land question in Zimbabwe: 145
    a) Pre-Independence legislation on land 145
    b) Post-Independence legislation on land 155

APPENDIX 2: 159
Response to allegations of deaths suffered during operation
murambatsvina/restore order 161

APPENDIX 3: 165
Quoted public opinions on the contentious relations between
Zimbabwe and Britain 167

APPENDIX 4: 177
My letter to Michael Ancram MP and letters from Andrew George MP, Peter
Bottomley MP, Andrew Hopkinson and Anne McIntosh LL.B MP . . . 179

Glossary 205
Bibliography 209

ABOUT THE AUTHOR

Mr. Zimi Roberto was born in Angola, Africa in 1958. He became refugee at the age of 3 when his parents escaped from Portuguese colonial oppression to the neighbouring Congo/Kinshasa in 1961. In Congo/Kinshasa (which afterwards was renamed as Zaire and currently as Democratic Republic of Congo) Zimi attended his primary and secondary schools and college in a Belgian educational system. He returned to Angola before it gained its independence from Portugal in 1975. From 1978 he was trained and worked as an Angolan national security officer for some years. Between 1981 and 1982, he received a further military preparation and took an introductory study in Marxism-Leninism at a Cuban military school located in Santiago de las Vegas, an outskirt of Havana, Cuba. He arrived in Britain in 1989 after returning to a civilian life. In Britain he first attended different colleges in London where he took a number of short courses and trainings. Between 2000 and 2003, he attended Ruskin College Oxford, and among other subjects studied, the most relevant to him were his introductory studies in writing for publication, cultural studies, European Union and radical political economy; he spent 2 years at the University of Oxford (Dept. for Cont. Education) studying Social and Political Science (Sociology, Politics and Economics), and also spent another 3 months taking an intensive short course in International Human Rights and Refugee Law at the same university. Mr. Zimi Roberto is currently the Director of a newly established organisation called 'Angolan Humanitarian Mission - UK', based in London.

ACKNOWLEDGEMENTS

When writing a book became my only alternative to broadly express my indignation with regard to the British contemptuous approach to Africa, particularly, the British aggressive foreign policy towards Zimbabwe, my great anxiety was related to English not being my first language.

However like every author, I have to express my gratitude to many people from different social backgrounds, particularly those countless Africans with whom I had exchanged experience about Africa's crucial problems, and could indeed learn much more from them. I also have to acknowledge my indebtedness to many other people who gave me words of encouragement to embark on this enterprise.

I have to thank officials at Zimbabwe and Namibia High Commissions, who kindly allowed me in to have critical and useful discussions with regard to the crucial and bitterness question of land in both countries, and made available to me some important documents on land policy reforms that have been taking place in southern region of Africa.

Nevertheless, my thanks are extended to all those British Members of Parliament and other officials, who took the interest and time to reply to my letters and share with me their knowledge of Africa's problems.

FOR ALL PEOPLE VOICING AGAINST THE NEW FACE OF
WESTERN IMPERIALISM

INTRODUCTION

In essence, this book concerns my individual anger and protest against the current British dirty foreign policy towards Africa in general, and in particular against the fuelling imperialist and neo-colonialist bellicose language towards the current Zimbabwean Government employed by some vicious British politicians at Number 10 Downing Street and Westminster. Therefore, I ask readers to forgive me for the anger-rushing mistakes that can be found in some of my letters sent to a number of British MPs/politicians, which are published in this book. However, this book is much more aimed at the general public rather than at the academic in the normal sense. This is a self-publishing enterprise and I sought no assistance in the course of writing this book. Generally speaking, to understand the essence of this book, I recommend readers to first concentrate critically on this introductory part.

I also want to draw attention of the readers to the fact that when I conceived the idea of writing this book in the course of 2004 and 2005, I was still living in England as an African citizen from Angola. Further to its completion, I became a British citizen. This means throughout this book, readers will obviously notice that I wrote parts of this book as an African citizen, and most of my letters to British MPs/politicians, published in chapter two of this book were also written in the same way.

Anthony Charles Lynton Blair 'Tony Blair' and George Walker Bush seem to assume that their 'GIANTS' nations have an international legitimacy to change any unfriendly or detested regime in the world of weaker nations on humanitarian grounds and in the name of God. In respect to Africa, the long consensus among aggressive British politicians is to see President Robert Gabriel Mugabe of sovereign Zimbabwe out of power. Hence, if for example, reports to the British intelligence claim that President Mugabe has an imminent plan to launch serious attacks on white farmers not in **"45 minutes"**, but, in **'45 hours'**, it is feasible that Mr Tony Blair, after being briefed by the British intelligence service, will rush to the House of Commons to persuade the very same aggressive parliamentarians who supported him in the war in Iraq, and proclaim to them that the threat in Zimbabwe is real. But, will his aggressive and persuasive language be convincing again? ***"It is a right thing to act now rather than doing nothing"***. Here, it should not be forgotten that Blair's conspiratorial pretext of **"45 minutes"** was what took the United Kingdom to an illegal and worldwide condemned war in Iraq in March 2003 – a historical and political blunder for a 21st-century British Prime Minister.

After many years of observing and understanding the pattern of British international politics, I initially thought that there was nothing I could do about some British politicians' conceptual blindness of Africa's reality and lack of critical understanding and assessment on what has been happening in Africa, particularly on what has been happening in Zimbabwe and why it has been happening. But as the time went by, I have come to understand that there was a need for me to be continually vigilant and informed of the British foreign policy development in Africa.

Therefore, the eloquent move to write this book came to me (in the course of years 2004 and 2005) after I wrote to 50 British MPs/officials, including the British Prime Minister Mr Tony Blair, expressing my indignation and worries with regard to the current British foreign policy towards Africa, particularly an aggressive British foreign policy towards Zimbabwe – aggressive British foreign policy based on accretions, distortions and misjudgement about Africa's reality. On the one hand, analysing the contents of the many responses that I have received from British MPs/politicians, I have concluded that there are many pompous British MPs elected to Westminster who seem to believe that they are the ones who know of everything about Africa than Africans themselves. On the other hand, I realised that the alarming culture of ignorance or disorientation and lack of interest in British foreign policy which tend to become monumental within British society, have created room for reticent and disingenuous British politicians to make people believe that everything that has been **thought, explained and decided in Western perspective** with regard to the Third World **MUST** be judged positive, rational and irrefutable.

As the aim of any book is mostly to provide insight in a given subject matter, thus, this book is an attempt to shed light and rescue ignorant or disorientated people to open their eyes to what blinds them about Africa's reality – rescue them from the belief that Britain has just been a benevolent nation – a nation which throughout history, its people have been going around the world to broaden civilisation in the blessing of a superior way of life and liberating alien peoples from their tyrannical rulers. For this reason, with regard to Africa, focusing particularly on Zimbabwe's case, this book addresses, criticizes and gives some straightforward and substantial responses to British MPs/politicians' imperialist bogus accusations of Africans and misrepresentations that obscure the core causes of the current contention between both historical and sovereign nations, Zimbabwe and Britain. Iraq's development is also referred to as a reminder/reference, and an example of a good lesson to be learned by all of us.

When I first conceived the idea to write this book, I was well aware that the events in Zimbabwe and other parts of Africa have been researched and published through a plethora of books found in the Western markets and library bookshelves. Even at the time I begun this undertaking, I had on my table a variety of written material covering virtually many recent major issues about Africa. During the gestation period of this book I knew that many British Parliamentary debates on Africa, and particularly on Zimbabwe, had been taken place and many British press reports on Zimbabwe's social and political crises had already been published. But, in looking at many reports on Zimbabwe, I noted that no interest has been attached to Africa's historical facts. I noted that some reticent British officials and biased British journalists are still bound to the lasting legacy of not revealing Africa's reality. I also realised that many of those reports and personal letters from British MPs on Zimbabwe have been the accretions and distortions based only on land reform policy, human rights and democracy concerns, and the political trouble that has consumed people of Zimbabwe during the Zimbabwe 2002 election – less or even nothing has been said with regard to the economic sanctions against Zimbabwe, masterminded outside of Africa. These are economic sanctions which for many years have been affecting millions of ordinary Zimbabwean people, who directly or indirectly are encouraged by the Westminster to rally against their legitimate and elected Government. In addition, less or nothing has been emphasised on the causes of the bitterness and suspicious relations between Tony Blair and Robert Mugabe, a factor that has actually stagnated an optimistic fresh move to the restoration of good and mutual relations between the two historical and sovereign nations, as many African leaders envisage. Whose fault is it? Blair does not talk to terrorists and dictators; however, he can visit Northern Ireland and China, but not his former colony, Zimbabwe.

Furthermore, I also knew that the land issue and the Lancaster House agreement of September/December 1979, also known as the '1979-Lancaster House Agreement' have been critical concerns in Zimbabwe. Lamentably, many press' reports published by the British media and many discourses by British officials have concealed or failed to explain further to the British public all developments about the '1979-Lancaster House Agreement'. Let us remember that after the Commonwealth Heads of Government Meeting (CHOGM) in Abuja, Nigeria, from 5 to 8 December 2003, the South African

President has made some crucial statements in which he blamed Britain and other Western powers as being responsible for the inevitable violent land redistribution in Zimbabwe. He also indicated that Britain was playing human rights issues to protect white farmers and change the regime in Zimbabwe. These statements will be discussed further in this book.

These facts and others are not taken into consideration by British media and British officials when making representations about the political and economic situation in Zimbabwe. Although the media has to tell stories as they are without worrying whether they may comfort ones and discomfort others, what we see too often, journalists tend not to be objective and totally impartial, because they also attach their own interest and perspective on the way they want to project their news and attract their readers and viewers. Let us imagine how a Western journalist who has relatives or friends who have settled in Africa would investigate and present to the British public an article on land redistribution which is taking place in a southern African region, particularly in Zimbabwe. Journalists dig out not for good news but for bad ones that attract the public. In these circumstances, some reports can be manipulating, distorting and misrepresenting of the real facts in Africa. Western media has been accused of double standards which can promote or destroy any individual or government should it prefer to do so – however, overall, British media is an insidious and harmful institution. When Mr Tim Yeo, a Conservative MP, was involved in an extramarital affair in the earlier nineties, he stated categorically in the *Independent* newspaper: *"Newspapers print stories they believe their readers want to read"*. Additionally, at London School of Economics, on 24 April, 2006, when delivering a speech entitled 'The news we deserve', Mr Charles Clarke, former Secretary of State for Home Office, told his audience that: *"pernicious and even dangerous poison"* exist in the British Press.

In view of all this, although writing a book came to be my only alternative to broadly express my concerns and views in a wide public arena, this book is not an attempt to dig-out-the-relevant historical facts which might have been already known to the public or alter Africa's history, it brings to light some of Africa's realities that are hidden to many people through the Western misrepresentations of Africa, through distorted British foreign policy towards Africa, particularly through New Labour's obscure and draconian approach to the current Zimbabwean Government.

Also, based partly on a wealth of many letters I have received from British MPs/politicians on Africa's affairs, this book attempts to expose the persistent Western imperialistic endeavour in Africa; expose the imperialistic language used by some British MPs on the current situation in Zimbabwe, an African nation that has become so special to Number 10, Westminster and the British media because of its land reform policy initiated in the 1990s. Less-informed people will obtain a better understanding of the root causes of the current contentious relations between Britain and Zimbabwe; the '1979 Lancaster House Agreement', the constitutional arrangement out of which Zimbabwe emerged as an independent state in 1980 – also, a constitutional arrangement out of which the UK pledged to provide funds to assist with peaceful land redistribution in Zimbabwe.

History is learned not only through academic books and lectures, but also through a first-person account by simple recounts, narration and chats that pass around from one generation to another within established communities; also through the film and music – it was through a music by the famous Congolese musician Luambo Makiadi, nicknamed 'Franco' that for the first time in the 1970's I heard about land problems in Rhodesia/Zimbabwe. Whereas, although part of this book is about my personal experience and first-person account, and the fact I have hardly tried to get this book published within up-to-date, and working at speed to keep pace with fast changing, I cannot therefore rule out the risk of being challenged for omissions and inaccuracies leading to some people being disappointed or even being offended.

Although some material contained in this book may assist scholars in one way or another, however, this book is not intended for academic purpose, and of course, many readers will note that I have chosen to write some parts of this book in basic English to meet the diversity of reading and understanding needs of different backgrounds of readers, particularly of those from non-English speaking countries with little knowledge of English language.

Yet, this is an important book which does not deal with fiction and emotions, it deals with real facts and goes straightway to the points which can shed light and rescue many people from their ignorance or disorientation of Africa's reality. But I also want to clarify to the readers that I have no snobbish disdain for my fellow decent British people of any background – I deeply appreciate their faithfully and unconditional generosity to foreigners – their genuine and faithful humanitarian help to the needy people around the world, particularly to those in Africa – my sincere gratitude to all decent British people who have been and are now on the fields, to directly assist people in need worldwide. I also recognise that there are many decent British politicians who genuinely work in the direction of mutual respect and co-operation with other nations for the benefit of the world community. By saying British aggressors in the House of Commons, I simply refer to those who supported Blair and Bush in an illegal war in Iraq; to those who believe that military action against weaker nations is the best option. For this reason,

I alert the readers to be very careful that any term used in this book, such as British people, British politicians or MPs is not intended to generalise, instead, intended only to those who consciously understand that criticism, remarks and so forth, are specifically directed to them. Hence, where I can, I will try to remain positive, consistent and objective in my remarks and my understanding and perspective of African continent.

Finally, this is perhaps a distinctive kind of book that many readers have not read yet, and more than anything, it has been elaborated on my own experience and understanding of British foreign policy and Africa's reality – it is therefore my sole responsibility for the interpretations and conclusions I have reached in the course of writing this book.

Arrangements of this book:

Before I tackle the first chapter of this book, I have first elaborated 20 relevant questions that added to the introduction will give the readers a clear idea of this book.

I propose to kick off the first chapter of this book with the development from the December 2003, Abuja Commonwealth Heads Of Government Meeting (CHOGM) to Blair's retreat from his "regime change" in Zimbabwe – Blair's imperialistic endeavour for "change regime" in Zimbabwe, while African leaders devote a great deal of efforts to a peaceful political solution in Zimbabwe, thus, undermining the Africa Union's endeavour for a unifying Africa. The second chapter brings some crucial statements made by Prime Minister Tony Blair, Presidents Thabo Mbeki and Robert Mugabe, and as to why British MPs are furious at Mugabe and Mbeki. It also exposes some extracts from British MPs' personal letters on Zimbabwe and some extracts from my personal letters to British MPs and concluding with further comments. The third chapter reviews research that explains to the readers, particularly ordinary African readers, how some British parliamentarians manifest their lack of interest in Africa. The fourth chapter focuses on serious criticism directed to some reticent and disingenuous British parliamentarians and other officials on British foreign policy towards Zimbabwe. Appendix 1: Re-publishes the bitterness and long-lasting land question in Zimbabwe: a) Pre-Independence legislation on land. b) Post-Independence legislation on land. Appendix 2: Re-publishes the response to allegations of deaths suffered during 'Operation Murambatsvina' (Restore Order). Appendix 3: Re-publishes quoted public opinions on why Zimbabwe matters for Africans. Appendix 4: Letters to and from some British MPs. Then, glossary and bibliography will follow.

WHO IS RIGHT?

To assess who is right on the current contention or to understand what has been happening between Westminster and Harare, and also to grasp what has perhaps going on in Blair's mind in his frantic and controversial last mandate as British premier, I thought it proper to elaborate for readers 20 pertinent questions (questions that form the basis of this book) that Number 10 Downing Street and Westminster would not provide straightforward answers:

1. Does Blair's comprehensive aid package to Africa mean another division of Africa between the prosperous allied and the non-prosperous African nations, a paving way for his "regime changes" plan in Africa?

2. After his historical and political blunder over Iraq, is Blair now simply seizing Africa's poverty as his last opportunity in Number 10 Downing Street to claim his best place in world history?

3. Why should Blair exclude Zimbabwe and other African nations from his comprehensive aid package to Africa, if for example, Portugal was not excluded from American "Marshall Plan" at the time of its brutal military dictatorial regime that eventually was militarily overthrown only in April 1974?

4. Why disingenuous British politicians advocate the "no" aid to undemocratic and corrupt African governments without explaining the origin of Africa's corruption – and who has created and supported African dictators during the Cold War period?

5. Do all British parliamentarians understand that land was a supreme Africa's cause for which African people paid with their blood and deaths

during the African colonial liberation struggle?

6. Since colonial era, the backbone producers of food in Zimbabwe have been black Zimbabweans. Hence, what did Michael Ancram mean by disdainfully expressing that "when we left [Zimbabwe] there was enough food... "?

7. Do all British parliamentarians understand the mind of President Roberto Mugabe, who had served 10 years imprisonment under the Rhodesian white minority regime led by Ian Smith?

8. Is it wise for British politicians to make people believe that President Mugabe is just a daft African old man, who one morning woke up and told his ZANU-PF members and supporters to go out and violently re-possess land from white settler farmers?

9. If mistakes (not crimes against humanity) have been committed by the Zimbabwean Government on land reform policy and on other domestic policies require British "robust/resolute action" and UN intervention, then, how about Blair's conspiratorial pretext of "45 minutes", which has already killed and continue to kill thousands of innocent Iraqi civilians, especially innocent Iraqi children?

10. Why not a resolute action against Bush's disastrous domestic policy that led to the tragic loss of more than a thousand of lives (overwhelmingly poor black people) in the aftermath of the Katrina hurricane?

11. Are the people of Zimbabwe, Africa Union and United Nations inviting Blair to change a regime in Zimbabwe?

12. On what grounds under the international rule of law can Britain decide the legitimacy to change any regime in Africa or elsewhere?

13. Has "regime change" in Zimbabwe, advocated by some British elites and aggressors, a genuine high moral ground of freeing poor black Zimbabweans from the West's so-called tyranny of Mugabe?

14. Are Africans pleased to see any African leader being humiliated in the eyes of the world by their former colonial masters as Saddam Hussein was toppled in humiliating manner by his aggressors, Bush and Blair?

15. Why is it that before land reform policy came into effect in Zimbabwe, President Mugabe had been a distinguished African guest to the UK, and

honours, decorations and privileges were bestowed on him by the United Kingdom?

16. Why has Zimbabwe become such a special African country to Westminster than it should be, and actually receives much of bad media coverage in Britain than any African country?

17. Are British politicians properly scrutinised by British people on what they claim about Zimbabwe, as they are now scrutinised with regard to the justification given by Blair to follow Bush in his illegal war in Iraq?

18. How can it be comprehended that those aggressive Westerners, who in the past ignored the human rights of black Africans and supported tyrannical regimes across the Third World, become the champions and lecturers of democratic and human rights values to African veteran revolutionary liberators of their people from an appalling historical human existence?

19. Have Western liberal democracy and human rights advocated in the UK and US after the Cold War ended in the favour of the West in 1989-1990, become the Western weapon to undermine the sovereignty and self-determination of countries run by leaders detested at Westminster and White House?

20. How a British Prime Minister, Tony Blair, who in the run up to war in Iraq, pompously did not listen to the very strong appeals which came from African leaders, especially from prominent African figures, such as Nelson Mandela and Reverend Desmond Tutu, begging him not to follow Bush in his war in Iraq without the United Nations' mandate and an international endorsement – and how that same aggressive Prime Minister could turn to the very same Africans to give them lectures on rule of law, liberal democracy and human rights values, and additionally, seek support of the same African leaders for a "regime change" in Zimbabwe?

CHAPTER ONE

ONE

HAS BLAIR RETREATED FROM HIS "REGIME CHANGE" IN ZIMBABWE?

To begin with, I propose five noteworthy points:

1.   Any African leader who invokes sovereignty and national self-determination to close the doors of his/her country from Western imperial ambitions as North Korea does should know that these international principles do not work anymore. In the new world order designed by the US and UK, sovereignty and self-determination of independent nations are no longer important values rather than Western liberal democracy and human rights values. Blair has always envisaged "regime change" in Zimbabwe to topple his African implacable enemy, President Robert Mugabe. However, the African total resistance to Western imperialism and neo-colonialism in Africa has forced Blair to rethink over what level of resentment he would provoke in Africa, and particularly in the southern African region, if his aggressive behaviour turns Zimbabwe into a failed African state.

2.   Among many reasons, African leaders' strong opposition to Blair's draconian approach to the Zimbabwean Government is duly justified for two reasons alone: (a) The South Africa apartheid, which was condemned worldwide, was not settled by the UK invasion of white minority government; (b) Ian Smith's regime in Rhodesia, which hijacked independence from the UK in 1965, was not overstepped when President Robert Mugabe (along many other Zimbabwean patriots) had already been arrested by Smith's regime in 1964 and served 10 years' imprisonment for making a so-called "subversive speech" – the white minority regime was allowed to continue by default until the London 1979-

3

Lancaster House negotiations that led Zimbabwe to independence in 1980.

3.   Blair and his supporters must learn the lesson that the doctrine of attacking weaker nations of the world on the pretext of human rights abuses or imminent external threat to the UK (**45 minutes**) has in fact been more subjective to many aggressive politicians at number 10 Downing Street and Westminster than of the real and present threat, factor that has dramatically damaged the credibility of both the moral and rational superiority of the West. Immoral and unjustified US–UK-led pre-emptive military intervention against world weaker nations will only come at a cost to their own people at home and abroad, as has already been experienced.

4.   Any tarnished and aggressive British Prime Minister, who takes his or her country to an illegal and unpopular war, will not leave Number 10 Downing Street proud hearted and dignified. If a PM wants to achieve a memorable place in history, there is no better example to follow than that of Sir Winston Churchill, one of the most respected British Statesmen, who on May 8, 1945, declared to the British people that Europe was finally at peace. The long war was over, and the streets of Britain resounded with joyful celebration.

5.   The Secretary-General of the United Nations, Mr Kofi Anan, has publicly declared the US-UK led invasion of Iraq as an international illegal war. Lured by Bush, Blair's madness behaviour which encouraged military invasion of Iraq on the pretext of **"45 minutes"** and evidence fixed to fit his aggressive ambition is unforgivable. This behaviour is intended to pursue his personal power and prestige on world stage regardless to the loss of thousands of innocent Iraqi lives and putting British people lives at risk of pitiless terrorist attacks as has now been experienced in a peaceful city of London. This is an offence of high crime deserving high punishment. The majority of opinions from all over the world indicate that Bush and Blair 'BB's' do not deserve memorable places in world history – they also MUST be brought before a criminal court where death penalty is applicable as the recent case of their implacable enemy Saddam Hussein.

It is sensible for people in the international community to ask why Mr Tony Blair is still allowed to talk about moral issues on world stage. This fact is what strikes me most. In my viewpoint, Mr Blair cannot talk to people anymore about moral values. If there is a need for African leaders or Africans in general to take from Western politicians some lectures on how right or wrong something is or on accepted moral standards such as respect for human rights and international rule of law, I now strongly believe that Mr Tony Blair has missed his advantageous historical occasion for his name to be included in the list of Western lecturers of these international moral values.

Before elaborating further on Mr Blair's draconian foreign policy against Zimbabwe and President Mugabe – foreign policy that sought to impose on world weaker states its will through punitive action such as embargo, sanctions and invasion, it is appropriate to refer to some established Western historical facts and figures that have probably been confusing to British Premier: he might have thought that going to war would make him a stronger British Premier and stronger statesman in the international sphere. I also want to establish some central reasons that ultimately might force Blair to rethink on his intrusion in Africa's affairs, particularly the strong resistance by the Africa Union 'AU', forcing him to retreat from his plan for "regime change" in Zimbabwe – a Machiavellian conduct which the President of South Africa, Thabo Mbeki never joined.

It was not just a contemptuous act, but madness behaviour of a rationale Prime Minister who was lured by Bush to encourage military invasion of Iraq on the pretext of **"45 minutes"** and evidence fixed to fit his aggressive ambition, after demanding and failing to secure a new UN resolution. By following the intransigent Bush to his war in Iraq, perhaps Blair was being confused with the traditional relations between the United Sates and the United Kingdom. The British Prime Minister was confused with those so-called traditional and special relations that existed between Winston Churchill and Frankly Roosevelt and Margaret Thatcher and Ronald Reagan. Given the originality of their social and political thoughts and actions, in British history, Churchill and Thatcher will remain authentic personalities and the British twentieth-century icons. Blair is not one of these excellent and inspiring personalities – he seems not to possess a clear moral vision and an inspiring and charismatic quality found in those 19th and 20th centuries prominent figures such as Mohandas Karamchand Gandhi, Nelson Mandela, Desmond Tutu, Haile Selassie I, Martin Luther King, Diana Princess of Wales, Bill Clinton, Fidel Castro (by resisting the US embargo for more than 4 decades, Castro has set out a model to be followed by the weaker nations of the Third World),

Rafael Guevara de la Serna (Che Guevara) or Ernesto 'Che' Guevara Lynch de la Serna, Mother Teresa and many others whose individual roles alone have brought remarkable and positive change in the national and international levels. Although it appears that Both emulate others, Blair and Bush, who have been attracted by the world for wrong purposes, should remember that President Ronald Reagan knowing too well the worst implications of an unjustified war, he had managed to win the Cold War without entering into a direct military confrontation with the former Soviet Union.

Being a follower of Bush (a wounded lion that in the forest attacks anything which moves around it), and endorsing the American tradition of world supremacy, the world does not offer Tony Blair, who is more like Bush than Bill Clinton, a dignified place in history. The past cannot be changed, and what is already known is that Tony Blair has no good past in history of his foreign policy. As we can contemplate a good future, for Blair to mitigate the overwhelming international anger on his aggressive foreign policy, the best place to start with after being out of Number 10, is to invite George Bush to establish a charitable organisation and continue his suspicious enterprise in fighting for African cause and the eradication of Africa's perpetual poverty – the advocated Blair's international humanitarian mission: 'Make poverty a history'

As weaker nations in the Third World are able to resist the US manipulating foreign policy, the UK has now become a volunteer follower or a "yes" country to the US. **"British people should stand shoulder to shoulder with American people"** – A relevant example is that of Venezuela in Latin American under the leadership of President Hugo Chavez, who came to power through a landslide victory in presidential election in 1998. Many people have been asking whether this is really the true sentiment? In Europe, in the political context, George Bush had the full and unconditional support of an unusual loyal friend, the British Prime Minister, Mr Tony Blair, whom he could easily motivate in heading for one of the remarkable blunders in the history of America and the United Kingdom. By invoking his famous words of assurance to George Bush, that "*The British people should stand shoulder to shoulder with American people*", Tony Blair has expressed his willingness to follow Americans in their new project of pre-emptive strike, meaning on every American dangerous and immoral mission around the world. It is important that the British people understand that any leader whose purpose of committing the national army to unpopular foreign invasion of other nations and that makes his or her own people vulnerable to terrorist attacks or hatred worldwide, as innocent people of America and United Kingdom experience nowadays, is tantamount to the offence of high crime. Thus, it has to be endorsed that a good leader should be the one, who always avoids controversial projects, be it in the domestic or international context. A good leader is the one who serves in the domestic and international affairs with clear ideas and goals – a passionate listener, a compromising leader in settling international disputes in the sake of the majority opinion and avoiding unnecessary loss of innocent human lives.

When Blair came to power in 1997 he was believed to be the man gifted with exceptional intelligence drive and an ardent problem solver in domestic and international spheres. This is not the case since he has become a liable Prime Minister: he failed to combat and reduce crime and anti-social behaviour as pledged in the Labour manifesto in 1997; he faced an embarrassment over accusations of running a parallel Labour Party within the party; he admitted to his wrongdoings as Prime Minister over involvement in the peerage scandals-secret loan issue to the Labour party without telling the party treasurer, Mr Jack Dromey; the alleged offer of peerages in return for cash or loans – honours up for sale is a matter of deep concern that has made him a problem himself instead of a problem-solver; while Blair turns to African sovereign states to seek good governance, demolish corruption and remove President Mugabe from power, he himself has become the first British Prime Minister in the history of British politics to be under police investigation over loans cash fraud/loans cash in return to peerage; his failings concerning Iraq and his attempts to become both international judge and litigant mean that he has become not only an international problem himself, but also a new liberator of alien people turned into international villain; the Prime Minister who helped George Bush to change a regime in Iraq and seeks now "regime change" in Zimbabwe, faces himself a regime change within his own Labour party; the Prime Minister who desperately appeals to African leaders to force the elected President Mugabe to step down, he himself has been clinging to power at number 10, despite of being so politically tarnished and exhausted; The Prime Minister who in 1997 when he came to power was believed by many of us that at the end of his mandate will enter in the list of the greatest British Prime Ministers, has popularly been forced to leave office before accomplishing his third full term, leaving behind him a mix of legacy: courageous and proficient political team leader who has done fair enough in the transformation of British public service and economy, articulate British political performer, but a man who only goes one way and reluctant leader in accepting or apologising for social, political and economic mismanagement or simple mistakes that have been occurring in the domestic affairs; an international undemocratic/dictator who does not compromise with other so-called world dictators; a war criminal who defies and undermines the authority of the United Nations; a British Premier who thought that could whenever influence and secure "regime change" everywhere in the third world, now knows it too well that it is almost certain that he himself will be out of Number 10 Downing Street before his targeted African enemy President Robert Mugabe;   the Premier who at the outset appeared to have no shortage of words and explanations on all his policies, and also showed the courage to face any situation and anyone inside and outside Parliament, has now been refusing to meet and dialogue with ordinary people – the grieving families who have lost their dearest in the war in Iraq, a Blair's war based on conspiratorial lies. In view of his disdainful conduct with the British public in the course of the 21st-century, Tony Blair, the partisan of reason, has also become an illegitimate vanguard defender and promoter of ethical and moral values on national and world stages.

However, do not underestimate the Prime Minister Tony Blair – he is not a "quite man", like Iain Duncan Smith. A tactical Blair knows about all this already, and also that time is running out and that there is little room left for political manoeuvring; he is aware that arrogance of power in the British political system deserves nothing but its complete eradication. He knows that people in the West, who believe that they are endowed with those supreme human qualities to run this world, cannot simultaneously be the same ones who fail the world. He also knows that something has to be done in terms of his change of attitude. It is therefore why Blair is hardly attempting to re-invent himself in many ways to deflect the world's attention to his remark-able historical and political blunder over Iraq. Long before talks on peace and security in that Arab country, and well aware of the frightful consequences of the unilateral US/UK-led disastrous and worldwide condemned illegal and criminal war that has already consumed many thousands of innocent Iraqi lives, and in an effort to impress the British people and the world, in his frantic last mandate at Number 10, Blair, this new British liberator of alien people, seizes on Africa's poverty as his last opportunity to achieve his ambi-tion of claiming his place in world history. That is the reason why Blair may have turned to Africans to pledge what he calls a "comprehensive Africa's aid package" through writing off billions in African debts and doubling aid to the continent. However, Blair has not yet made any comprehensive state-ment that explains in simple terms the root causes of Africa's poverty that he is keen to defeat in his last mandate. He seems to regard Africa's poverty and inequalities rooted in the colonial system as if they were caused by a natural phenomenon or unintended man-made mistakes. However, Blair has sought the support of his companion of war Mr George Bush for his comprehensive African aid package, the prerequisites of which they have agreed to be good governance and eradication of corruption in Africa. These requirements can only be interpreted with caution by many African politicians as some regimes in the continent have already been placed on his blacklist for "regime change" through this Machiavellian aid plan. For many Africans, there is a compelling reason to suspect that Blair's initiative for establishing his Commission with some Commissioners from his own Labour party to help Africans defeat poverty cannot be genuine. From what Blair's behaviour revealed to us in the run up to war in Iraq, I doubt that he would prefer to help Africans rather than imposing to them his own will and device on how to run their continental affairs. It would be understandable when on January 14, 1977, Mr Robert McNamara, the president of the World Bank, announced to the world his initiative leading to the creation of a commission consisting of world experienced, respected politicians and economist experts. He initially made it clear that the proposed Commissioners should be totally independent rather than being official representatives of governments and should work independently to put together what he called "basic proposals on which global agreement is both essential and possible"; work impartially and faithfully for the restoration of good relations between North-South, leading to people's progress and prosperity in the two sides. Therefore, the former German Chancellor, Willy Brandt was asked to lead the new 'Independent Commission on International Development Issues`, a project that subsequently expanded to include more members from both the North and South. However, it was much more about a plethora of meetings, written papers, waste of time and money – and little has changed in Africa since the establishment of the Commission of former German Chancellor in 1982.

In relation to Blair's Commission, passionately, one argues this:

> Tony Blair wants to help Africa as he says, then here are a few
> things that he should consider. The root of Africa's problem is
> simple. It is the West! They're hypocritical, have too many negative
> propaganda about Africa, do not see Africans as real people with
> real issues, making Africans dependent on charity from the West is
> destructive. Will the West help Africans without exploiting them?
> We all know that the West does not do anything unless they are
> benefiting. Even to keep Africa poor, is a benefit to the West.

Although Blair did not deliberately include land issue and the cause of poverty in his agenda for Africa when he took the Presidency of G8 in 2005, he sought to have a fresh look at the crucial and immediate problems affecting Africa, problems such as relating to economy, education, health, the environment, HIV/AIDS, and so forth. Blair's fresh look at these issues can only be regarded as a gimmick to buy time in government and a serious mockery to Africans. These issues are not new to Western governments, British politicians, economists, British charitable organisations working in Africa, and many others. And the solution to them could not be achieved during last year of Britain's Presidency of G8. On Blair's Commission, Mr Peter Hardstaff of the World Development Movement stated that "This commission is a diversionary tactic designed to draw attention away from 30 years of broken promises on Africa." It is also crystal clear to Mr Blair that HIV/AIDS that has been devastating Africa cannot be regarded merely as a health problem, but a serious problem to the general development of the continent. The UN's policy document notes that: "the threat of AIDS may reverse decades of development, undermine economic growth, and unravel the social fabric that has held communities together during previous crises, demands a retooling of UN responses". Statistics by the Food and Agriculture Organisation show that "of the 36.1 million people living with HIV/AIDS, an overwhelming 95 percent live in developing countries". How many people will die in Africa before Mr Blair's fresh look gimmick? Since 1985, AIDS has killed about 7 million agricultural workers in Africa. It could kill 16 million more before 2020, this is according to the UN report. Is this information new to Tony Blair?

To my view, Africans no longer need a lecture on governance, democracy and human rights which have long been a strong excuse by the West, particularly by the US/UK to deflect people's attention from the real issues affecting the continent. I do not foresee anything new that Blair will expect of members of his new commission on Africa when they seek advice with expert thinkers, civil society and the public on the above issues. In his February prime ministerial press conference, Blair added that: "I believe Africa is the scar on the conscience of the world, and think it is right that we continue to treat this as an absolute priority over the coming years". Africans have listened to this pledge again and again, and it has become akin to boring Western music that they would not like to buy any more.

Blair should first reflect and ask himself: "how long it took him and George Bush to find billions of dollars and pounds that were invested in a just war in Iraq?' A war without any political and economic interests! Many billions of dollars and pounds were quickly allocated to liberate alien people thousands of miles from the United Kingdom and the United States of America. The US is an influential promoter and a major financial contributor of the UN, and therefore, it is believed that the US controls and forces the Organisation to devote more resources to specific countries of its own interests, turning blind eye to other in real needs, such as those countries in Africa. Having a large new investment injection, enough subsidies for black

African farmers, free and fair trade, no more selling of arms and landmines to Africa, it is feasible that in 5 to 10 years to come, Africa could be able to achieve dramatic improvements in social and economic spheres. If the life of black African people was valued at the same level as the life of people in the West, by now, there should be another "**Marshall Plan**" for Africans. The West would first give money to Africa, as Americans did to Europe without looking at democracy and human rights as prerequisite. When the financial package was delivered to Europe with the help of the Marshall Plan, for example, Portugal, which at that time had a dictatorial and fascist regime, was included. That regime was overthrown in April 1974 by a military coup.

After failing in the Arab world, Blair now turns with his vanity to help the suffering black Africans. After being in Number 10 for 6 years, the Prime Minister surprised many people in opening his 2004 February ministerial press conference by not blaming anyone nor explaining why, but recognising that Africa has been the only continent in the world to have grown poorer in the past 25 years. According to the economic statistics available to him, Africa's share of the world has halved in the generation; the continent receives less than 1% of direct foreign investment; 44 million children do not go to school and millions of people die as a result of famine or disease or conflict. Here, Blair did not emphasise what sort of conflicts, where and the main actors who cause them. Interestingly, Blair also came to recognise that Africa risks being left even further behind. The Prime Minister's compassionate idea was to establish a Commission for Africa that would take a fresh look at Africa's past, present and future – a comprehensible assessment of the situation in Africa and policies towards Africa. What has worked, what has not worked, and what more can and should be done, suggests that after Labour being in government for 7 years, and with huge Foreign and Commonwealth Office with Departments in each African region, and a Department for International Development undertaking work in Africa, the Prime Minister still does not know much about Africa. He assumed the presidency of G8 in 2005, and it appears that he still not yet know what has worked and what has not worked in Africa – but within the European Union, he remains a champion of economic and diplomatic sanctions against detested nations in the world, as he has done to Zimbabwe and its people.

Strong suspicion has been mounting in the sense that if his plan becomes a reality, Blair's neo-colonialist intention (before he leaves Number 10 Downing Street) for "regime changes" in Africa is first directed at only one African country. There seems little doubt that this country has to be the sovereign state of Zimbabwe led by President Robert Mugabe, and where Blair's long imperialistic intention has not attracted support among African leaders since the December 2003, Abuja Commonwealth Heads of Government Meeting (CHOGM). Therefore, Blair's consternation in Africa is not just about lack of good governance, lack of democracy and human rights values: instead, it is uppermost an incessant systematic Western imperialist control of the economies of the continent. It is very simple to understand this process if we retrace Africa's history since the 1884-1885 Berlin Africa Conference which led to a partition of Africa. This Conference, organised by Europeans to subjugate Africans, was the beginning of a Western system that has ever since played perpetually on the minds of Africans and continued to divide Africa for the sake of Western political, economic and strategic advantages.

Blair's Commission for Africa was established with 16 internationally notable personalities, and all 15 of them are from English speaking countries – from the United Kingdom, United States and Africa. It appeared that the Commission has deliberately ignored to include some leaders from French and Portuguese speaking countries from Africa. For many Africans, this is an indicative that Blair's Commission might have a tendency of prioritising economic assistance first to a selected group of African English speaking countries. This is an initial divisive character of a Commission akin to help Africa as whole.

Blair's famous Commission for Africa was constituted as follows:

Mr Tony Blair, British Prime Minister
Mr Gordon Brown, British Chancellor of the Exchequer
Mr Hilary Benn, British Secretary for international Development
Mr Michel Camdessus, former head of International Monetary Fund
Sir Bob Geldof, Irish musician, actor and political activist
Mr Meles Zenawi, Ethiopian Prime Minister
Mr Trevor Manuel, South African Finance Minister
Mr Ralph Goodale, Canadian finance minister
Nancy Kassenbaum Baker, former US Senator
Mr K.Y. Amoako, United Nations Economic Commission for Africa
Mr Benjamin Mkapa, President of Tanzania
Ms L.K. Mohohlo, Governor of Bank of Botswana
Dr Anna Tibaijuka, Director of United Nations' HABITAT, Tanzania
Mr T.J. Thiam, Group Director of Aviva in Ivory Coast
Mr William Kakema, chairman of Ugandan Manufacturers
Mr Fola Adeola, chairman of Fate Foundation in Nigeria

Blair's humanitarian project through his Commission for Africa could be another boring music for most Africans because of the previous plethora of established commissions, and their broken promises which led to little achievement in bringing prosperous life to Africans. What is known and what has been argued is that Africa would not need much of alms from the West if it opens its markets fully to African goods, particularly to African agricultural produce.

The following are the previous Commissions:

Brandt Commission established in 1982
Live Aid, held in 1985 to raise money for the victims of famine in
Ethiopia
Arusha Charter in 1990
Jubilee Debt Campaign in 2000
New partnership for African Development (NEPAD) established in
2001
Millennium Challenge Account (USA) established in 2001
Johannesburg Summit on Sustainable Development held in 2002
G8 Declaration in 2003
International Labour Organisation World Commission on Social
Dimensions of Globalisation established in 2004

Returning to a catalogue of British Prime Minister's failure, another problem with Blair is this: Blair's exaggerated sense of his own importance and a feeling of moral superiority to other people is clearly demonstrated in the run-up to war in Iraq and has been regarded by many people across the world as of an arrogant attitude. It is a dangerous political approach to the current handling of the British foreign policy by a modern and civilised British Prime Minister. Although it may not be always the case, however, one may well conclude that this attitude might have its roots in the old assumption that places the white race in a superior position not only to other races but might also be connected with the old Western idea which suggests that those who believe that they are endowed with human superior qualities are destined to rule all others, and those ruled have to submit to the rulers. Thus, on the one hand, this still obliges some people and politicians within Western modern and civilised societies to foster the belief that **everything that has been thought, explained and decided in a Western perspective has to be judged as right and rational.** On the other hand, everything decided in the West (particularly in the US/UK) should not be challenged or dismissed. For example, the US/UK lecturers of the Western liberal democracy, human rights and good governance in Africa cannot be challenged. Policies on how African leaders and the Africa Union would run African continental Affairs should be prescribed by the Western intellects, because they are the ones who are believed to know the proverbial "anything and everything" about Africa than Africans themselves. This audacious act of deliberated West's contempt aimed at disaccrediting the goodwill and authority of African leaders and the AU, feeds more the complicated and suspicious relationship that exist between Africa and the West. To arrogantly demand that all African affairs be conducted in Western mode is tantamount to telling Africans that they are not real people endowed with excellent human qualities to resolve their continental affairs in African terms. These old Western beliefs continue to give rise to lively polemics or discontentment felt within African societies, in which some Westerners still maintain banal and stereotypical notions that Africans still cannot govern themselves. President Mugabe appears to be justified when in an interview with a British journalist David Dimbleby emphasised this:

> We have not stopped singing to the theme of unity and love. Even
> the whites are free to live here. But they must change. Your kind
> – the British kind – are very difficult to change. We rate them as
> the most conceited, the most arrogant, the most selfish and the
> most racist in our society. I do not mean you Mr Dimbleby, this is
> not you in person – but the ones we have here.

Indeed, assuming the Western high morality and rationality, let us also not forget about Blair's lack of moral and political responsibility when he took our country to war in Iraq on the basis of his subjective political judgements of **"45 minutes"**. Let us not forget the trouble brought to the peaceful City of London by Mr Blair, a barrister educated at Oxford University, who ignored the fact that the United Nations was the only international body to mandate a military invasion of Iraq in accordance to its Charter. Yet again, let us not lose sight that Blair has just disappointed many people everywhere – and even when our kids at home have become overwhelmingly aware and upset of the consequences of war in Iraq, our British Prime Minister still courageously maintains and tries to have us believe him that the recent London terrorist bombings have not been the direct result of a unilateral US/UK-led illegal invasion of Iraq; the continuous appalling treatment given to Arab prisoners; Taliban/Al Qaeda dead bodies (burned) in Afghanistan by American troops; ill-treatment given to Iraqi prisoners at Abu Ghraib and suspect terrorists at the American Guantanamo Prisons. In addition, the mounting strong suspicion and accusations that British airports have been used by the CIA to transit (rendition) suspect terrorists to secret prisons run by the CIA across the world or run by countries where they are likely to be tortured. During the British Prime Minister last visit to the US, it came at great surprise to many people when both Blair and Bush 'BBs' took the courage to admit before American cameras and people that they have made mistakes over Iraq. Blair should admit his political blunder over Iraq first here to the British cameras and people. It is important that we remember that Clare Short and the late Robin Cook had previously told the new British liberator of alien people, the reluctant Tony Blair to publicly admit his political arrogance and mistakes over Iraq. History will reveal the rest of his arrogance and mistakes on his foreign policy.

Where is the so-called Western high moral ground? Where is the rationale of Blair and those aggressive British politicians who supported the illegal war in Iraq? It may be said that those who are believed to have those superior human qualities and high moral ground to run this planet are the ones who have been failing the world and losing high moral credibility. However, in this present situation, if one asks people in the UK and US if Blair and Bush can really provide sound advice on high morality and human rights values, let's say, to Presidents Mugabe and Mbeki, for some people the answer would be a "yes". But put that same question to the rest of the world, undoubtedly, the answer will be a definite "no". If the former answer is considered right, therefore, morality has its unique meaning in Western societies. There is no other alternative.

Considering what has happened with the intelligence on both sides of the Atlantic ocean, it is of paramount importance for British people to realise, and whatever the spirit of national patriotism, that only the ignorant and naïve will allow any British government to commit British men and women in uniform to another military invasion with pretext of crimes committed over 10 years, by someone in his own country thousands of miles from the US and the UK. It is also worthwhile to remember that Blair took our country to an illegal and unpopular war in Iraq after admitting he had not been briefed that the "**45 minutes**" claim was referring only to battlefield ammunitions. Therefore, let us consider what will happen if in future, someone, who desperately wants to see President Robert Mugabe out of power, comes to Britain and reports a fabrication to the British intelligence that Mugabe has an imminent plan to launch serious attacks on white farmers not in **"45 minutes"** but, in '**45 hours**', is it not possible that Blair with an aggressive posture will rush to the House of Commons and persuade the very same aggressive British parliamentarians who supported him in war in Iraq that the threat is real? Will his persuasive language be convincing again? ***"It is a right thing to act***

now rather than doing nothing". Subsequently, we all came to understand that Blair's persuasive words turned out to be arrogant and faulty, and deserving nothing but a worldwide condemnation. However, in some ways, there is no doubt that Blair is a good British political performer. These words of Mr Anthony Charles Lynton Blair will remain patent in my mind for the rest of my life and become a lasting memento of this Premier. It is also important that British people remember this moment in world history.

Let us move on. Blair's abysmal rush to an unpopular and illegal war in Iraq and to a counter-productive Iraq venture aimed solely at removing Saddam Hussein for being defiant to the international rule of law and a horrible Arab dictator, merely indicates his own importance, superiority and rationality over his own fellow British citizens. Blair did not listen to the millions of British people, particularly to those directly concerned families and relatives of the victims of the 9/11 terror attacks. The appeals from the UK and worldwide leaders against that unnecessary and costly war in Iraq have indeed fallen on the deaf ears of an arrogant British Prime Minister. Consequently, at the last general election, we saw how much Blair was humiliated – combined fact that will eventually precipitate his departure from Number 10 Downing Street as a weaker British Prime Minister, who has done reasonably well on domestic issues. Gifted with a good Cabinet team, Blair has undoubtedly done reasonably well on domestic affairs, even though when he entered Number 10, a well-established gigantic "welfare state" had already been put in place by preceding governments. As recognition of this, in my five-page letter to the Prime Minister, in January 2004, paragraphs two and three state:

> Before I move on to the main points of this letter, I would like first
> to say that I enormously appreciate and congratulate with the Prime
> Minister's performance of governing Britain and the British people,
> and I am satisfied that you have been doing fantastically well on the
> domestic agenda. From my own assessment, I am also satisfied that
> among other progresses made by the labour government during six
> [years] in power, the British economy is in good shape; I use to visit
> St Mary's Hospital, and I note that there is a considerable improve-
> ment, although more has yet to be done; Under the new deal, more
> young people have found suitable jobs; I welcome the introduction
> of top-up tuition fees, because it is right and sensible for people
> to make some financial contribution for their education, and as
> repayment of loan depends on the ability to pay, it is a tremendous
> advantage for graduates. Anyway, despite all this hard work, the job

is half done as you put it yourself, hence, it does not dispel some blames and criticism. Whereas, the kind of welfare state established with the arrival of Labour government in 1945, and its further expansion throughout the years following the end of WWII, has created a culture of dependency, making many people in Britain to ignore their individual responsibility and believe that they can get anything free from the government, otherwise they express their anger at the general elections. In meantime, on the domestic policy, you have been one of the most greatest and successful leaders of Labour Party. Well done Prime Minister.

However, as the Prime Minister may well agree with me and other many people in Britain and elsewhere, it is regrettable and disappointing that in handling the British foreign policy, you have been failing the British people, and as the result, you are now facing the political costs that you could have avoided if you had listened to your people not to commit British troops in war in Iraq without the mandate of the United Nations. Over Iraq, you have lost important members of your Cabinet, your poll rates have gone down while President George Bush retains his Administration intact and his poll rates have gone up since the capture of Saddam Hussein. The decision to go to war in Iraq with pretext of Weapons of Mass Destruction, which allegedly were an imminent threat to Britain was unfounded and an exaggerated fear or panic. What strikes me most is the fact that the Prime Minister was well aware that it was likely that many thousands of innocent civilian lives, especially children would perish in Iraq just because of one person, Saddam Hussein. Now, think about the physical and mental pain that Iraqi war has caused to Ali Abbass and other many Iraqi children. However, these are not the issues I intend to address further here, let me progress on the issues that affect my continent, Africa.

Paragraph eleventh adds this:

Furthermore, with regard to Zimbabwe, what most Africans have been arguing, and as you may agree with that, it appears that many British politicians, including the Prime Minister do not properly understand or ignore what is accommodated in the mind of African leaders, particularly of the generation of those who came to power after being involved in the liberation struggle to free their countries and people from colonialism; of those who had spent long years in prison and tortured by white rulers; of those who saw their fellow fighters' blood spilling on the ground or perishing in the bush during the long years of liberation struggle; of those who still remember their fellow black men lying in mass graves throughout Africa, as British people still remember their heroes died during WWII. Furthermore, they all commonly fought and liberate their people from common enemy (colonial rulers), therefore they regard themselves as revolutionary liberators, and again, commonly, they will soldier on - fight tactically anything they regard as being a form of neo-colonialism [regarded as neo-colonialist] propaganda to undermine their leadership. Whereas, it is well known that, in Africa, and in Zimbabwe in particular, the prevailing conception is that President Robert Mugabe first is a revolutionary libera-tor and hero, who had spent part of his best life time in prison under white masters and fought for the liberation not only of Zimbabwean people, but also for the liberation of other African nations such as Namibia and South Africa, including the fight for the release of Nelson Mandela and others from long years of Prison under apartheid regime. Hence, mobilising African leaders against Mugabe will have no significant effect due to African solidarity resulting from that common liberation struggle against colonial-ism and apartheid. It is also difficult for the Prime Minister to currently attract moral and political support from Africans against Mugabe, because you yourself did not even listen to strong mes-sages from President Thabo Mbeki and other prominent African public figures such as Nelson Mandela and Desmond Tutu, begging the Prime Minister of Britain not to follow the Americans to war in Iraq. Furthermore, using tough language and threats to Mugabe will only worsen the existing tensions in Zimbabwe, increasing the number of Zimbabwean refugees in [the] UK. In addition to this, it is extremely important for the Prime Minister to understand that Africa is not a Balkans or Iraq, Robert Mugabe is not Sloban Milosevic or Saddam Hussein. Africa is just a poor and pacific con-tinent which has been suffering for centuries, and a former colonial power dealing with African leaders with public threats would not be pleasant to most African people wherever they are living. And also, no African would be happy to see any African leader humiliated in the hands of the former colonial masters as the way the world saw humiliated Saddam Hussein - Or to see innocent people, especially those African children, who already have been suffering from poverty, starvation, diseases, etc to perish or be burnt or be amputated by the western bombs just because of one African leader detested by some politicians at Westminster and Downing Street.

Also, towards the end of my letter, the paragraph before the last states:

Prime Minister, the time has moved, and history has demonstrated that as people we need each other. Many British people feel comfortable to live in Africa, and many Africans would like to live in Britain and Europe. The Times newspaper - Thursday January 8, 2004 published: I quote: *"We're British and proud of it, say ethnic minorities - A CLEAR majority of people from ethnic minorities are confidently asserting their Britishness, government figures show"*. Therefore, let us put threats aside, let us all work hard together in order to make both continents better places for both of us and both benefit equally from the fruits of that hard work. Indeed, there are many decent British people who have been doing a decent job in Africa, they are welcome by Africans, and therefore, they should be free of [from any] fear and allowed to continue with their job rather than be jeopardised by the conflicting political relations between Britain and Africa.

My views of Blair are echoed clearly in the words of Clare Short (known now in the British media and British political circles as a woman of mass destruction), a former Labour Cabinet member/Secretary for international development, who also resigned over the Iraq row. This Former Cabinet member came to reinforce this line of pressure to make Blair admit mistakes over his fiasco in Iraq. She made it clear that she did not have any personal vendetta against the Prime Minister. She had no personal bitterness against him, but she felt that Blair's litany of misleading actions and his rush to an illegal and unpopular war with Iraq were inexcusable. According to Short, the best way that Blair could correct what has gone wrong, and clean up the Labour Government and go forward to confidently fight the next election (2005 election) would be to tell or persuade him to recognise that he has done some good, made some mistakes, but the time has arrived for him to step down for the sake of the reputation of the great British Labour party. The invasion of a sovereign nation of Iraq by Bush and Blair was not solely motivated by the humanitarian cause of liberating Iraqis from the tyranny of Saddam as the latter justification given by Blair when no Weapons of Mass Destruction (WMD) were found in Iraq. War for "regime change" and occupation was more motivated by the abundance of Iraq's oil supplies. This war has since been part of the Western struggle for economic and strategic survival.

Historically, the old and traditional British foreign policy has been to conquer, dominate and maintain its economic interests and British social values wherever in the world. During its long colonial and imperialist history, Britain, wherever it could, maintained its conquered interests through its military might. But as times changed, Britain also moved in adapting its foreign policy to those changes. As decolonisation became inevitable, particularly during the period after the Second World War, Britain, in a very carefully and orderly manner, transformed its Empire to a Commonwealth group of countries – countries with republic states and others retaining the British Monarch as their Head of State.

After Western imperialist greed had destroyed the lives and cultures of millions of Africans through slavery and while imperialists had concluded that the mounting pressure on abolition of slavery was an irrevocable process, they already thought about another exploitative plan of other parts of the world through a different system. It was no longer a question of exporting people from Africa to the plantation fields in America, but to exploit them locally. As a result of the European scramble for Africa, indigenous African people again found themselves disturbed by Europeans, who separated them through frontiers established in European capitals. The European contempt for human beings led them to separate Africans with no regard to their ethnic grouping or to other natural divisions. This partition was concerned solely with the economic competition amongst some greedy European imperialist countries, and also was aimed at transforming and maintaining Africa as a backup source of raw materials for the Western industries. Let us remember that when Japan surrendered at the Second World War, the first atomic bombs that America dropped on Hiroshima and Nagasaki were made of uranium that originally came from Belgium Congo. Additionally, Africa has also been the West's long markets for its technical services and manufactured goods, including arms and personal land mines.

Moreover, Mr Blair may be aware that in nineteenth-century Britain, the word imperialism was explained or argued in both ways: negative and positive. It was explained in the negative manner to describe a tyrannical government. It usually referred to Britain's neighbour, France. It was used in a positive way, when it described the British colonial policy of unity of its Empire. Others believed that imperialism was a synonym of being rational, influential and more powerful than other nations in the world. Therefore, in Britain, some people were proud to call themselves imperialists. They were completely wrong.

Blair and his disciples probably have not yet realised that whatever meaning or justification can be there, imperialism has not been a good thing in promoting human understanding in the relations between human beings. Imperial colonialism was a WMD to other people's cultures and traditions in many ways. Imperialism has always been a divisive force, which has since led people to inequalities, greed, suspicion, friction, resistance, nationalist emotions, racism, terror, human aggressiveness, revenge, rancour, wars, and much more. However, more interestingly, in the West, the historical gratitude to imperialism prevails nowadays. These include the following characteristic: the exportation of civilisation and the discovery of other nations; the exportation of Western technology and skills; the mercantile activities that brought close different people, and a general improvement in the standard of living worldwide.

In addition, looking at historical facts, it can be confirmed that British imperialistic policy will never be beneficial to all the people of the UK. It can only benefit a small group of people at Number 10 and Westminster and British capitalist multinational businesspeople, who go alongside with imperialist governments. The mere objective of Bush and Blair in their so-called pre-emptive action, and the spread of liberal democracy and freedom have been visibly seen as a pursuit of their own power and prestige. It has become clearer to many ordinary people that in this contemporary world, the US and UK humanitarian mission has not been about human rights values, but mixed with neo-colonial propaganda, economic strengths, and, of course, a continuous maintenance of American supremacy and preservation of strategic positions to maintain US global control. For this reason, of course, many states in the Third World (such as the case of Zimbabwe and Britain) have continuously accused their former colonial powers of neo-colonialism and approach their former colonist states with strong suspicion – sometimes unfounded suspicion with regard to their foreign policies, which in some cases have no imperialistic purpose.

The end of the Cold War in 1989/1991 paved the way to a new calculated form of Western imperialism and justification in intervening in other world weaker sovereign nations on the grounds of Western liberalism, particularly concerning liberal democracy and human rights values. This leads to a violation of the traditional tenets of self-determination of other nations.

I am now returning to the British Prime Minister in relation to his connection with the current Zimbabwe Government led by President Robert Mugabe. Foremost, the neo-colonial decision to overthrow President Mugabe's Government in Zimbabwe has been invoked by British aggressors – Blair and some British politicians at Number 10 and Westminster, not by African leaders and politicians. In respect to Africa, in particular to Zimbabwe, Mr Blair's perversity is to fight against the principles of sovereignty and national self-determination of African people, principles set forth by the West itself to give nations the right to make their own decision without interference from others. 'To make sense of this, it is broadly said that when Blair came to power in 1997, a draconian British Prime Minister, a man with no U-turn on his decisions, a new British hardliner politician who does not waste his time to dialogue with those who himself describe as dictators, and disgruntled with Zimbabwean Government land reform policy which has been regarded as a serious menace to British economic there, his connection with Zimbabwe was first to internationalise the bilateral contentious relations between both countries by mobilising his natural allies in the Commonwealth Club, some sections of US' hardliner politicians and some friendly countries in the European Union to isolate President Mugabe and impose baseless and unjustified diplomatic and economic sanctions on ZANU-PF. On Zimbabwe, it has been noticeable to many people that disregarding or paying no attention to the principles of sovereignty and national self-determination, for almost 10 years at number 10, Blair has been employing all Western imperialist and neo-colonialist tricks that never attracted support from African revolutionary leaders/politicians – vain and shameful tricks that have only met strong resistance in Africa as a whole, and particularly in the southern African region.' In his book called 'Political Theory – Second Edition – 1999, page 102', looking at anti-colonialism and post-colonialism, Andrew Heywood explains:

> … In a sense, the colonising Europeans had taken with them
> the seed of their own destruction, the doctrine of nationalism.
> Anticolonialism was thus founded upon the same principle of na-
> tional self-determination that had inspired European nation-build-
> ing in the nineteenth century, and which had provided the basis for
> the reorganisation of Europe after the First World War. However,
> anticolonialism did not simply replicate classical European nation-
> alism but was also shaped by the distinctive political, cultural and
> economic circumstances that prevailed in the developing world. In
> many ways, the desire to pursue a distinctively developing-world
> political course strengthened rather than weakened once indepen-
> dence had been achieved. Postcolonialism has therefore been drawn
> towards non-Western and sometimes anti-Western political philoso-
> phies…

According to many African people, the cause for the malaise between

Westminster and Harare is one. It is the Zimbabwe's fertile land. President Mbeki has been charging Britain and other Western powers for the inevitable consequences of the social, political and economic crises resulting from deliberate Western broken promises to a peaceful land redistribution in Zimbabwe, which in my own understanding were aimed at preventing poor black Zimbabweans (original landowners) from entering and competing with white farmers in the Zimbabwean farming industry, a way forward to alleviate poverty among Zimbabwean people that Blair is keen to rescue from long misery.

It is further important that politicians and people in the West not to forget that in a historical context, land issues were a core cause of the black liberation movements in Africa, particularly in the southern African region, where thousands of black people paid with their blood and deaths. It has to be acknowledged that land has been a bitter question at the centre of the bilateral dispute between the two historical and sovereign countries, Zimbabwe and the UK. The Government of President Mugabe has since complained that Blair and his Government have endeavoured to internationalise this bilateral contention by mobilising the countries of the European Union, some of the USA political sections, international business communities and friends within the Commonwealth to turn against the ruling Government of Zimbabwe. Complaints from Zimbabwean authorities go further to consider that, while enormous efforts have been undertaken by the Zimbabwean Government in the direction of a peaceful Zimbabwe and a gradual process of democratisation of the country, Blair and his followers insist to influence the removal of a government of a sovereign nation of Zimbabwe. The last peaceful and democratic 31 March 2005 parliamentary elections are evidence that Zimbabwe has been reforming in terms of democracy. To obscure or disaccredit this Zimbabwean democratic progress, politicians at Number 10 and Westminster have taken a step too far in engaging themselves in hostile neo-colonialist propaganda and a sustained Western's campaign of vilifying and demonising ZANU-PF in the Government and its President. Most of the comments made by British politicians (see second paragraph) tend to suggest that President Mugabe is a serious menace to British economic interest in Zimbabwe and President Mbeki is not doing things to British style or as Blair wishes.

Although many at Westminster feel proud of the British contribution towards land reform in Zimbabwe, among many African people, it is overwhelmingly argued, and as some writers have reinforced it, that taking into consideration the huge economic profits that the British Empire had made from Zimbabwe's fertile productive agricultural land, British financial contribution to equitable land redistribution in Zimbabwe could not be only £62 million of which £3 million has not yet been delivered since Blair came to power. This is a deliberate meagre sum made available by Britain on land distribution in Zimbabwe, when as a matter of fact the sum should be between a quarter and half billion of pounds. Let us remind ourselves that it did not take long for Tony Blair and his team to organise some billions of British taxpayers' money to be wasted on an illegal and unpopular war in Iraq – billions of pounds being wasted on killing innocent Iraqi people, particularly innocent Iraqi children. Let us also not forget how quickly the EU found around 50 millions of Euro to be granted to France following the recent riots. Among other Western countries, the UK alone **MUST** share the responsibility and blame for the social, political and economic consequences causing the suffering of millions of ordinary Zimbabweans that it pretends to liberate from President Mugabe. In a book called, *'Blood and Soil – Land, Politics and Conflict Prevention in Zimbabwe and South Africa - 2004'*, published by International Crisis Group, summary pages xi and xii state:

> When a Labour government came to power in the UK in 1997, a
> sharp chill developed in British-Zimbabwean ties. While much has
> been made of this, the following points must be made to put it in
> context. First, during the initial phases of land reform in the 1980s,
> a less cumbersome British approach to funding could have allowed
> far more land to be redistributed at a time when the Zimbabwean
> government actually seemed more committed to an equitable
> policy. Secondly, the sums spent by the British on redistribution
> were remarkably low [£62m] given the historical benefit the British
> Empire gleaned from Rhodesia's fertile land. Thirdly, the sometimes
> bellicose language employed by British aid officials was counterpro-
> ductive...

The Government of Zimbabwe has made it clear that while it strongly believes in the empowerment of the black majority across the economy, it will not tolerate those who are used as fronts by whites to derail the land reform programme. President Mugabe does not hide his position on the land issue in Zimbabwe. He has since maintained that there will be no compromise, because land has been the most important challenge that his government has yet to accomplish. In his own words, Mugabe affirms:

> When I went to prison and I spent all those years in exile during
> our struggle, I did it to get our land back - and that is precisely
> what the war veterans are doing. I mustn't be seen as negating

myself.

President Mugabe is determined to pursue the land issue to his last day, as notable Zimbabweans did for him previously. ZANU-PF website recalls this:

"Land should be given to its rightful owners"-Chirimanyemba-
John Taviringana Chirimanyemba, a centurion who witnessed whites when they invaded, conquered and seized land in Zimbabwe and later emerged as an advocate of the liberation movement, advancing the idea of resisting the unjust political, economic and social subjection has one wish before he dies, to see land given back to its rightful owners.

It is crystal clear and a matter of principle that the land redistribution programme was inevitable to correct the imbalances in land ownership rooted in the Zimbabwe colonial era. However, it has also been pointed out by many people inside and outside of Zimbabwe that the current Government has made some mistakes of judgement as to whom the land should be given. Zimbabwean Government officials have openly recognised this misjudgement too. Redistribution of land to some black Zimbabweans with no previous link or experience of agricultural farming has been one of the factors leading to food shortages in Zimbabwe. This mistake has been recognised by members within the Government. But, British politicians also should take into account the reports from the 2003 IMF (International Monetary Fund), the 2002 USDA (United States Department of Agriculture) and the 2004 UN, explaining that the devastating food shortages since 2000 were largely to be blamed on the severe drought. In 2003, Mr Ismaila Usman, IMF's Executive Director for Zimbabwe, asserted that the drought was the worst in 50 years, and appealed to the IMF to give Zimbabwe another chance. Also, diseases were among the flood of problems facing Africans, diseases such as the exterminating HIV/AIDS which is regarded as a serious obstacle that affects the African labour population, and hence impairs African economic development and prosperity.

Many of us will recall that, following the Commonwealth Heads of Government Meeting (CHOGM) in Abuja, Nigeria, between December 5 and 8, 2003, on his arrival back to Britain from his anti-Mugabe campaign in Abuja, on December 9, 2003, the British Prime Minister rushed to the House of Commons to enthusiastically report on Zimbabwe. In reporting to the House, Blair insisted on "regime change" as a sole solution to Zimbabwe's political and social crisis, thus, he went on lecturing Zimbabwe's neighbouring countries not to support Mugabe and his regime. Instead, according to Blair's arrogance, Zimbabwe's neighbours should consider reconciliation in the direction of removing President Robert Mugabe from office. In his own words, Blair stated:

> It is in interests not to support Mugabe and Zimbabwe's regime, but to facilitate national reconciliation in the interests of changing regime.

At the time that Blair was lecturing African leaders about the benefit to be brought within the Southern African region by removing their veteran comrade of Africa's colonial and apartheid liberation struggle, President Robert Mugabe from office, I did not realise that it was Blair's indirect pressure on President Mbeki to intervene in Zimbabwe on his behalf.

On his campaign for Zimbabwe's indefinite suspension from the Commonwealth, Blair, who also counted the support of the international community, the well-known "GIANTS" of the Commonwealth, Australia, New Zealand and Canada, was happy to see that this pre-planned suspension had worked. He paved a way to press for "regime change" in Zimbabwe subsequently, alongside his natural allies. In this context, one may argue that foreign policy decisions which have been taken in the UK automatically become a circular for Australia, New Zealand and Canada because they all share the same world view. This picture of conformity leads all of them to behave in the same way and they can go to illegal and unpopular wars together. Additionally, on international affairs, they all take the same stance and put pressure on the same language, and they all agree on punitive actions such as sanctions against targeted world weaker states.

On a sovereign African state of Zimbabwe, Blair has his own formula which has not been explicit if national reconciliation, leading to "regime change", would be done through the same procedures as the one which took place in South Africa in 1994, where the people of South Africa went to the polls for the first time and changed the minority apartheid regime to a majority rule. He has been lobbying African leaders for support to topple President Mugabe, but what he probably had not realised, and what is abundantly clear to many people, is the fact that Blair is now regarded an aggressive British Prime Minister, who in the run-up to war in Iraq, pompously did not listen to the very strong appeals which came from African leaders, especially from prominent African figures, such as Nelson Mandela and former Archbishop Desmond Tutu, who begged him not to follow Bush in his war in Iraq without the United Nations mandate and an international endorsement. Now, haw can the very same British Prime Minister, Mr. Blair, who after his fiasco in Iraq, and after becoming less trusted in his own continent and adding condemnation after condemnation from almost all the world for unnecessary loss of thousands of innocent lives in Iraq, turn to the very same Africans who have begged him not to go to war in Iraq, to give them some lectures on liberal democracy and human rights on Zimbabwe, and therefore seek their support for a British military invasion of Zimbabwe? Is it not a political immaturity for a modern British Prime Minister in international politics? Is it not Blair's contempt for veteran African leaders, particularly for President Thabo Mbeki, who runs the most complex society on the earth to be told or reminded by Blair of an African benefit resulting from "regime change" in Zimbabwe?

How can an aggressive Prime Minister of a former colonial power become an adviser on human rights values to Africans, who, had faced with incalculable sacrifices; who could fight bravely and bring a dehumanising colonial imperialism in Africa to an end; who courageously could free their people from an appalling human existence and still continue to fight for the recognition of African people's rights and dignity, which had been denied to them for centuries by the very same people who have now become the new West's liberators of alien people and champions of paradoxical Western liberal democracy and human rights values? Why is it that Blair and his associates cannot hesitate to use neo-colonialist propaganda of indecent words to characterise those who resist the permanence of imperialist political and economic control upon Africa as a single objective of the West in the continent for centuries?

Whether Blair and his accolades like it or not, it must be revealed to the British public that most African leaders, in particular, those of the Southern African Development Community (SADC) will agree with President Mugabe's stance on land issue and support him to correct the wrongs of British colonial history. And President Mugabe has made it clear to Westminster and Number 10 that there will be no compromise on land issue, because it has remained the major single problem his Government has yet to put right for the benefit of the black majority people of his country. As a matter of principle, it is a sensible thing to do. Independence and dignity are values that had been lost during Western European conquest and domination of Africa. The struggle for the total conquest and restoration of these values under the new phase of Western neo-colonialism has been a common struggle for Africa as a whole. And what is happening in Zimbabwe is exactly the continuation of that struggle to regain these lost fundamental rights of Zimbabweans, despite the superiority of Western imperialist and neo-colonial propaganda machine.

Blair's accounts on Zimbabwe to the House of Commons, and the debate that followed it, have led me to become increasingly suspicious and apprehensive that he could again use his arrogance of power to mislead the British Parliament. He might manipulate the British people as he did with Iraq, and eventually change a regime in Zimbabwe through a British military invasion. For several times, in the House of Commons, Blair invoked "regime change" in Zimbabwe as his best devised new approach to resolve the current crisis between the two countries, without further explaining to the House and the British people the root causes of what he perceives as the persistent political, economic and human rights chaos in that African country.

In addition, Blair does not understand that his deliberate disregard to the fact that land was one of the supreme African causes for which African people died for will never make him popular man in Africa. This is an indisputable reality. And, although he seemed not to realise that the hiccups on Zimbabwe by most African leaders during the CHOGM have been an embarrassing blow to him, however, he proceeded in giving his accounts to the House of Commons on Zimbabwe and his own formula to redress Zimbabwe's political crisis without addressing the land issue. As stated earlier in this book, Thabo Mbeki's words have been ignored by many pompous British politicians, when he blames Britain and Western powers for causing a land crisis in Zimbabwe.

Dishonesty is not a characteristic of the successful and powerful leader; instead it is a recipe for ultimate abysmal failure. Apart from being unable to explain to the British people the root cause of the contention between Britain and Zimbabwe, Blair's doctrine of "regime change" of the sovereign weaker nations to be adopted in Zimbabwe, has obviously attracted words of support from quite the same aggressive British parliamentarians who have supported him in the controversial and illegal war in Iraq. Some MPs have advocated the Western new values of democracy, human rights and good governance recently exported to Africa, values that are merely enforced when the UK political and economic interests in the continent are at stake or when long-term control over Africa has to be maintained. Some suggested that such actions and options were all aimed at finishing with President Robert Mugabe as quickly as possible.

Again, *"It is a right thing to act now rather than doing nothing"*.

These words of Tony Blair to the British Parliament when he was presenting his case for war in Iraq cause tremendous fear to many weaker nations and world leaders who are not welcomed at Number 10 and Westminster. But it is not clear when the White House and the Westminster assume that Libya relinquished its nuclear programme at the time President Saddam Hussein was toppled because of President Mu'ammer Gaddafi's (Mu'ammar Gadhafi) fear of facing the same fate. Although Iran insists on its nuclear programme for civil purpose, its authorities are aware that their country has always been an implacable enemy of the White House and in the face of a US/UK-led invasion and occupation of Iraq, Bush's administration will press Iran to follow Libya's path. Authorities in Syria accused and warned to halt supporting and providing havens to terrorists who scare the world, are not greatly different from the Iranians.

Let me come back to the case of Libya. It has been officially declared within the White House, Number 10 Downing Street, Westminster and Whitehall that the pre-emptive attack on Iraq that led to the removal of Saddam Hussein from power has forced the Libyan President, Colonel Mu'ammer Gaddafi to surrender the country's Weapons of Mass Destruction (WMD) for UN inspection. The exercise has worked. But my working hypothesis is that this presentation is too obscure and misleading, and is aimed at regaining the hearts and minds lost by Bush and Blair worldwide after their unilateral invasion of Iraq, an Arab country. Given the long bitterness and litigious relations between Libya and the US, I am inclined to draw the following conclusion: Libya represented unfinished business for the Republican Government under the late President Ronald Reagan, who had failed to kill Colonel Gaddafi in a US bombing raid (April 15, 1986), and Saddam Hussein represented unfinished business for the American administration under the former American President George Bush senior, Bush's father. The man to accomplish all these assignments was their Republican junior President, George Bush.

However, a military attack by a giant Western nation against a small nation in Africa was officially justified by the late President Reagan as reprisal for what he termed Libyan "state terrorism". Therefore, as a form of punishment, it was regarded by the US administration as a just and rational decision. The bombing raid that failed to eliminate the Libyan President, took the lives of many innocent civilians. The outrage was a matter of deep regret, and was also regarded as a US act of terrorism by the international community and under the international rule of law.

Mr. Blair is aware of self-inflicted political trouble and endless worldwide popular pressure that has amounted since his political misjudgment over the Iraq invasion. This misjudgment was a result of his own arrogance in handling the Iraqi alleged WMD contention, and the formidable political cost of joining Americans to a unilateral war against Iraq. Taking these events into consideration, Mr. Blair was well aware that after the removal of President Saddam Hussein, an action that many US people supported in compensation for the pain inflicted on them by 9/11, Bush could move quickly and eventually invade Libya to finish the job that one of his Republican predecessors could not accomplish successfully. But, Blair might have fully acknowledged the political and economic costs that the Iraq war has caused and continues to cause the Labour Government and Britain, factors that narrowed Labour's victory at the last general election. Mr. Blair has found himself in very difficult position after he has offered assurances to Bush through his famous message of solidarity: *"British people should stand shoulder to shoulder with American people"*. This message has been interpreted that Britain would fight alongside Americans anywhere in the world, regardless.

Where Libya is concerned, Blair realised that he could not afford to follow America in another unpopular war. Indeed, it became evident at that time that the absence of WMD in Iraq had to have a negative effect on Blair and the Labour party at the last general election; however, in relation to Libya, he took a cautious position and played this political game differently with Bush. Blair wanted to get a third mandate in number 10 and accomplish it fully, as he has become now the long-standing Labour Prime Minister to hold office for three consecutive mandates. His ultimate political ambition is to overstep the legendary Margaret Thatcher. In this situation, according to my working hypothesis, what Blair perhaps did, was to order a series of secret meetings between British and Libyan officials to reach a compromise that, on the one hand, could satisfy Libya and, on the other hand, would give assurances to Gaddafi that Britain would do everything possible to prevent Bush from invading Libya. I believe that the surrender of Libya's WMD to the UN inspection did not concern Gaddafi's fear based on what happened with Saddam Hussein, as has been explained and perceived in the West. Instead, it implied that Blair did not want to be seen as a follower of Bush in another unilateral and costly war under pretext of a pre-emptive attack against another rogue state that supports or harbours terrorists, a rogue African state suspected of possessing or having a programme of developing WMD that could end up in the hands of terrorists and others. Britain's compromise with Libya led Gaddafi to relinquish his WMD ambitions, which in essence was more beneficial to the British Government, particularly Blair, who has been struggling to repair his tarnished image at home and abroad, mainly in the Arab world. Additionally, a tactical Blair found himself without any room to manipulate the British Parliament and the British people by claiming that the "threat is real" and then again using his persuasive words: **"it is a right thing to act now rather than doing nothing"**. Now, let's see what will happen with Iran (US implacable enemy country).

Libya's deal with the UN also benefits more Western businesses which have already been rushing to Libya in search of fresh contracts in the exploration of Libyan oil, gas reserves and other resources worth billions. The Anglo-

Dutch energy giant Shell has already signed an agreement to invest millions for a search of new oil reserves. The aircraft and defence contractor British Aerospace (BAE) has been in contact with Libya to pump million-pound deals to supply civil aviation equipment.

The so-called secret negotiations between Libya and Britain have the approval of many Africans. Even though my working hypothesis is accurate and whatever happened behind scenes, President Gaddafi made a courageous and rational decision at the right time to save the lives of Libyan's innocent civilians, especially innocent children from those bombs which have already killed and changed the lives of many Iraqi children, as in the well-known case of Ali Abass. It is important for African Governments to advance democracy and show respect for the basic principles of human rights, as these are the Western excuses for interfering in continental affairs or for not providing enough aid and cooperation for development and prosperity in Africa.

Furthermore, any settlement of a dispute between Western and African nations must satisfy both sides equally. In this context, it is well to remember that among African supreme responsibilities, African leaders are expected to redouble their efforts to resist any form of neo-colonialism and imperialist domination, and use whatever lies in their power to fight for the complete freedom and self-determination of African people. Well done Colonel Gaddafi!

Moreover, in Africa's context, Blair still makes reference to Sierra Leone. When the Secretary-General of the United Nations, Koffi Anan, summoned the international community to help in Sierra Leone's civil war, Britain under Labour party was the first and only European country which promptly sent in troops in 2000. During Sierra Leone's civil war, 1000 British troops were initially sent to help with the evacuation of foreign nationals. Although the British Ministry of Defence and politicians insistently claimed that the British forces that were being dispatched to Sierra Leone had the only task of evacuating British nationals, and not being involved in direct military confrontation with any local forces - but once on the field, there were involved in provision of logistical support to the discouraged UN forces, and also involved in training of government forces. The British troops' direct involvement in that civil war led first to the total control of Sierra Leone's capital city (Freetown) and its airport, and subsequently, alongside the local government forces, the British troops also assisted in the capture of the rebel leader, Foday Sankoh, forcing Sankoh's rebels of the RUF (Revolutionary United Front) to retreat to the bushes. In a vain hope, Blair has expected and impatiently waited for a UN call for the international community to intervene in Zimbabwe on humanitarian grounds and liberate Zimbabweans from the so-called tyranny of

ZANU-PF and Mugabe. This UN call never came to Number 10 Downing Street.

However, let us remember that historically the traditional British foreign policy has been to conquer, dominate and maintain its economic interests and British values wherever in the world. Let us not be distorted by this British involvement in Sierra Leone, which appears to be benevolent because one might have already argued that this generous action to save lives in that former British West African colony cannot be regarded as genuine. It brings us to the reminiscence of Rwanda's genocide in 1994, in which more that a half-million people perished in the eyes of the international community that Britain is an active member. Why a generous Britain did act promptly to prevent or save lives during that 1994 Rwanda's genocide? The answer is simple: Sierra Leone is linked historically to Britain as its former colony - Rwanda is not - Sierra Leone is abundant with diamonds gifted by nature, Rwanda is not - and these minerals were at the core cause of the country's civil war. The final reflection of all this is that whatever justification is given in the West, Africa was divided into West European powers to remain a source of raw materials for the Western industry The end-goal of the Berlin Conference was the European pompous act of annexing a huge African continent for the development of Western capitalist economy and prosperity of people in the West.

In relation to Zimbabwe, I happened to worry too much about President Robert Mugabe. When they show the President on British TV, viewers are practically guaranteed bad news about him. Although he always looks smart and confident, I was wondering if he really has been listening to the rancorous comments and vicious threats from Number 10 and Westminster, and if he really takes them seriously. However, surprisingly, Jack Straw, former British Secretary of State for foreign policy had once announced in the House of Commons that Britain will not send troops to Zimbabwe. Although it appeared to be a mixture sense of relief and delight, but I strongly doubted that a cautious and vigilant African leader like President Mugabe would allow himself to be deluded by Straw's statement, the British Foreign Minister who openly stated that the results of last Zimbabwe's parliamentary elections were seriously flawed, while both the South African and the African Union missions concluded that the election reflected the will of the majority of Zimbabwean people. In his own words, Straw added: "I can't be too obvious about what it is that I find so disturbing about the election. So I announce that the election did not reflect the will of the people of Zimbabwe when in fact what I really worry about is that the election did not reflect my will". During his time as British Foreign Secretary, Jack Straw was perhaps an ignorant or never reflected on the fact that there is no government in the southern African region which came to power from colonial revolutionary liberation struggle or armed rebellion e.g. the case Ugandan Government led by President Yoweri Museveni that has been defeated through free election.

President Robert Mugabe has always rated Mr Tony Blair as a British imperialist and neo-colonialist, and has also publicly accused him of setting gay gangsters towards his person to protest against the alleged human rights abuses in Zimbabwe. President Mugabe's approach to gays has been a kick in the teeth to the British gay rights campaigner Mr Peter Gary Tatchell, who in particular claims that giving children more sexual rights and education will help protect against abuse better than a British Megan's Law. Tatchell is a British citizen who on 14 March 1995 was labelled by the Daily Mail paper as a 'homosexual terrorist'. Sometimes ago, in European capitals, namely London and Brussels, Tatchell took a personal risk in ambushing the President of Zimbabwe in an individual protest with regard to the alleged human rights abuses in Zimbabwe and subsequently, in a bizarre and vain hope of performing a citizen's arrest, in Brussels, Belgian capital, he attempted his own citizen's arrest on the President, which resulted in him being beaten and left in coma by the President's body guards. Now, people would expect the famous British gay activist, brave and hero Tatchell to turn to Russia, and ambush the high ranking Russian official, the Mayor of Moscow (capital city of Russia) Yuri Luzhkov, who has very recently viewed gay rights marches as 'satanic'. The Mayor also added: "Moscow came under unprecedented pressure to sanction the gay parade, which cannot be called anything other than "satanic".

The events in Iraq are still fresh in our minds, but I have been worrying too if Mugabe still remembers them or has made available some videotapes of the humiliating end of Saddam Hussein. I wonder if he still remembers what happened to Nicolae Ceausescu of former Czechoslovaks and Samuel Doe of Liberia, and the recent case of Charles Taylor, former President of Liberia who is attending an international court of justice in his own country. I am also certain that Mugabe remembers how the powerful man in the Balkan region, the late Slobodan Milosevic, was driven from Belgrade to the International Court of Justice in The Hague for committing crimes that offended the moral conscience of mankind. But I came to understand something and I do not refute the broadly held African view that Mugabe has not been worried about some British politicians' accusations and vicious threats because he knows how to deal with such matters. He also knows perfectly well that for several reasons, he differs from the above dictators whose power ended in a humiliating way: First, he is certain that despite being despised by Westminster, most Africans understand that he has been resisting his former colonial masters, whose in Zimbabwe, have been protecting their white settlers "kin and kith" and their economic interests; Zimbabwe's Government had complied with the 1979-Lancaster House Agreement on the 10 years' constraint land redistribution following the independence of Zimbabwe in 1980. It means that the constitution elaborated in London in 1979 stipulated that the new Zimbabwean Government was prevented to start any land redistribution for 10 years from Independence date. The Land Reform policy came into effect only 10 years after Independence date, when the Zimbabwe's Government felt that it was no longer constrained by the 1979 political agreement on land distribution. Second, most African people, particularly politicians, blame Britain and other Western powers for being responsible for Zimbabwe's social, political and economic problems. Third, Zimbabwe has no WMD to be deployed in **"45 minutes"**, and it does not support or harbour terrorists who can cause a real threat to British interests anywhere; the Zimbabwean African National Union-Patriotic Front (ZANU-PF) is not itself an imminent threat to British interests, except a threat to Zimbabwe's occupied land; Zimbabwe never invaded its neighbours or any country – Zimbabwe does not involve in illegal invasions of other nations (Zimbabwe along other south African countries intervened in Democratic Republic of Congo at the request of its government); Zimbabwe does not have any prison to be compared with the American Guantanamo Bay prison or Abu Ghraib prison in Iraq established and run by American occupying forces; Zimbabwean Government does not run secret prisons around the world for torture of suspected international criminals nor are its airports used to transit (rendition) international suspected criminals. Fourth, Zimbabwe still retains its membership in many international organisations; Zimbabwe is a full member of the UN and enjoys support of the majority members of the organisation; it retains its full membership in Africa Union (AU); Southern African Development Community (SADC); Non-aligned Movement (NAM); Group of 77 (G77), Africa, Caribbean, Pacific (ACP; Common Market for Eastern and Southern Africa COMESA; and it entertains excellent bilateral relations with China; Zimbabwe's resistance to its former colonial power is regarded as a good cause that attracts unconditional African support and solidarity. Fifth, and more importantly, the good news is that in time, with the international and domestic pressure concerning Blair's fiasco in Iraq, Mugabe knows that British people are becoming more and more cautious about what politicians at Westminster claim about Zimbabwe. Finally, after his ZANU-PF landslide victory in the recent Parliamentary elections, President Robert Mugabe has announced his planned triumphant retirement in 2008. 'ZANU-PF's plan or proposal to adjourn the 2008 Zimbabwe Presidential election to 2010 is a sole matter for the Zimbabwean Parliament to discuss and reach a conclusion. Here is a simple example of Venezuela. Very recently the Venezuela's President Hugo Chavez asked his Parliament and the country to be allowed to rule by decree. After a series of debates in the Venezuela's Parliament and in the country, eventually, the President was granted new special powers after an extraordinary assembly vote in the main square of the capital, Caracas – vote that allows him to rule by decree for the next 18 months. Due to Blair's contemptuous and aggressive approach towards ZANU-PF, I strongly doubt that Mugabe would think of stepping down while Blair is still British Premier. It would be regarded as he has conceded defeat over pressure from the current Number 10 Downing Street.

It is important to realise that many African leaders, particularly the two of Troika mandated by the Commonwealth to deal with Zimbabwe's crisis, Presidents of South Africa and Nigeria, Thabo Mbeki and Ollusegun Abasanjo have been devoting enormous effort to see the ruling ZANU-PF and the Zimbabwean main opposition MDC (Movement For Democratic Change) parties and, in general, the people of Zimbabwe reconcile their differences and come together to resolve all their current internal problems. Even when the SADC member-countries have expressed their strong indignation to the extended suspension of Zimbabwe from the Council of Commonwealth, the new Western liberator of alien people, Mr Blair, the mastermind for Mugabe's removal from office, jumps in to viciously invoke "regime change" in Zimbabwe, reinforcing the persisting Western disdain for Africans, aimed at undermining Africans' endeavour in the direction of a peaceful solution that would prevent Zimbabwe from becoming a failed state in the southern African region. The removal of ZANU-PF from power by Britain military invasion or complicity would lead to an African nationalist guerrilla's warfare that will turn the country to something relatively similar to what is happening in Uganda, Democratic Republic of Congo, Sudan and Somalia, where no effective government has been established since 1999, and so forth.

Given the obtrusive expatiation by Westminster that avoids emphasizing on the 1979-Lancaster House Agreement, many people across the UK and Africa have now possibly begun to understand or even agree with President Thabo Mbeki, who insists that Britain has been causing the Zimbabwe's land crisis. If Zimbabwe's situation, as British politicians claim, was on account of Mugabe's oppressive regime, economic mismanagement, abuse of human rights, lack of freedom of press, Mugabe's rigging of the 2002 Presidential election, and so forth, by now, we would expect Tony Blair to change all regimes in Africa and elsewhere. Is there any government in Africa which does not control in one way or another the national media or is there a country in the world with a clean record on human rights?

As the new international humanitarian liberator, why does Blair or his Westminster's followers not invoke "regime changes" in Burma, where a military regime has been allowed to continue to suppress the opposition political parties and the people of Burma? Aung San Suu Kyi, Burmese human rights activist and political leader, inspired by the non-violent practices of Mohandas Karamchand Gandhi and Martin Luther King, and despite becoming a national hero and an international icon, she has been in political trouble since 1989. Suu Kyi won the Nobel Prize for peace in 1991: She was placed under house arrest in 1989, albeit, her party, the National League for Democracy (NLD) won the 1990 general election in Burma. Since then, the Burmese junta military regime refused to give up power and held Suu Kyi under house arrest until 1995. She was detained again from September 2000 until May 2002, during which time the NLD had secret negotiations with the junta in an effort to break the political deadlock. In May 2003, she was once again detained, taken into "protective custody" as confrontations between the NLD and government supporters increased, but now, she is again under house arrest. Additionally, there have been alarming reports on Burma's summary executions, murder, rape, starvation and systematic destruction of villages by military junta forces, and hundreds of thousands of ordinary ethnic minority people are forced to live in the remote jungle, escaping government oppression. In light of this fact, in my view, and of many fair-minded people, the Westminster humanitarian purpose has to concentrate first in Burma rather than in Zimbabwe, where, Mugabe has been uncompromised on land redistribution and this being the cause of long bitterness between Westminster and Harare.

Another factor that should be recalled here is that when something emerges in the UK or elsewhere, which does not comfort British politicians or undermines the British credibility, the language used at Westminster and Number 10 is this: "let us forget about it and move on". Whereas, I have to draw the attention of my Right Honourable MPs at Westminster and my readers to *The Times* Saturday, January 24, 2004, page 2, which states that the Prime Minister's wife Cherie Blair, recognises that George Bush had stolen the 2000-US presidential election:

> Although the Prime Minister was pragmatic about Mr. Bush's victory, Mrs. Blair was far less sanguine about the Supreme Court decision that gave him the keys to the White House. She believed Al Gore had been "robbed" of the presidency and was hostile to the idea of her husband "cosying" up to the new President. Even as they flew to Washington for their first meeting with the presidential couple, Mrs. Blair was in no mood to curry favour, the book '*Anthony Blair: the Making of a World Leader*', by Philip Stephens states:

> Cherie Blair still believes that Bush had stolen the White House from Gore", he wrote. She asked more than once during the journey why they had to be so nice to "these people"... "The book's disclosures of Mrs Blair's forthright views will cause embarrassment in Downing Street, because of Mr. Blair's good working relations with Mr. Bush, and the Foreign and Commonwealth Office, although they will not surprise officials or ministers who know her well. She is known for expressing her views forcefully in private.

More interestingly, although with all technological advancement in the electoral system process in the US, irregularities were common and were outlined to the British media and Westminster with regard to the 2000-US election fiasco. With regard to Zimbabwe, it is obvious to recognize that in many Third World countries, the electoral system has always been problematic because of the lack of sophisticated electronic systems. However, Number

10 and Westminster have continued to accuse Robert Mugabe of rigging the 2002 Zimbabwean Presidential election. On the Zimbabwe 2002 election, Blair and his associates never said "let us forget and move on". Instead, it remained as Blair's pretext for "regime change" in Zimbabwe. For Blair and his accolades, "Mugabe must go", has been the prize phrase, despite opposition from most African leaders. All governments may make mistakes in their domestic and foreign policies, and Zimbabwean Government has openly expressed its regret for some few incidences which have resulted in loss of life during the land crisis. It has also been taking measures to crackdown those who took the advantage of land crisis to acquire land illegally. The measures have also been forcing those government officials who dishonestly acquired more than one land to return back the rest to the government, and those who do not comply are liable to be charged with theft offence. However, Blair has hijacked this Zimbabwean old matter to continue to press for possible imperialist assault on weaker and sovereign nation of Zimbabwe.

Many British politicians in the House of Commons expect President Thabo Mbeki to press President Mugabe to step down, and by doing otherwise, Western critics have also tried to undermine his leadership. In Africa, it is well endorsed that President Mbeki is exerting a political maturity that must be expected of a South African president, and in my view, what he has been doing with regard to Zimbabwe is conventional international politics. President Mbeki has no international legal mandate to impose or dictate what the Government of Zimbabwe should or should not do. But as a president of a sister country with a common history of struggle against slavery, colonial oppression and apartheid, and within the international norms, he can only advice, suggest, and so forth, but not invoke imperialistic language of "regime change" in Zimbabwe. Zimbabwe is internationally recognised as a sovereign nation and the politics of that country is a mere internal affair of Zimbabwean people.

Blair and his associates attempt to override Africa's history, and deal with Africans and their crucial social problems with no reference to history, like a medical doctor who unprofessionally attempts to treat a heart patient without fully investigating that patient's family medical history and the development of the disease. For Blair, a cure for Africa's problems, as is suggested by his own's approach, has to be through strong and lengthy lectures on liberal democracy and human rights values to African leaders, values for which Africans themselves paid with blood and deaths during the struggle for black African people's dignity as human beings; the fight for freedom and liberty denied by the very same people who have become the forefront defenders of the black African cause.

According to what is known, the reason for "regime change" in Zimbabwe put forward by aggressive British politicians has been concerned with a lack of respect for political democracy and human rights in Zimbabwe under Robert Mugabe. In contrast, and according to many fair-minded Africans, it has become obvious that democracy and human rights recently advocated in the West have been regarded as a tricky subject in the political relations between Africa and the West. Many African people and politicians argue insistently that the post-Cold War human rights pressure on African governments represent the West's most fashionable weapon that undermines those African leaders who do not comply with the wishes of the USA and the UK. To sustain this perception, just after the December 2003 CHOGM in Abuja, Nigeria, in his weekly electronic letter in his party's website journal, ANC Today, President Mbeki stated again:

> Britain opposed Zimbabwe's readmission to the commonwealth this
> week merely to protect its "white settler, colonial kith and kin. And
> that western powers are using the demand for Mugabe to respect
> human rights merely as a tool for "regime change" in Zimbabwe.

Arriving at this point, what more has Blair left to tell Africans? Perhaps, his best address to Africans might be akin to the following words: In the West, we understand that during that dehumanising African colonisation, the civilised West did not respect the human rights of indigenous black Africans, and even when the '1948 Universal Declaration of Human Rights' came into effect; black Africans were subjected to degrading human conditions, arbitrary imprisonment and torture; black African women were raped by Western colonist soldiers; we did not act promptly when Ian Smith hijacked Rhodesia's independence in 1965, because we had avoided confronting our "kith and kin". Never mind, these are things of the past! Continuing, he would need to add that, recently, we, the US and the UK have invaded and occupied Iraq on Western high moral ground, not on the fear of Weapons of Mass Destruction, and as we were wholly committed, we have successfully removed that Arabic evil dictator from power. We (Bush and Blair) have established an Iraqi court and Britain provided a further training to Iraqi judges who charged Saddam Hussein of crime against humanity and sentenced him to death by hanging in November 2006. Without any delay, and in the eyes of the entire world, the Arab dictator who came to power in 1979 and took control of all Iraq and its citizens, was eventually executed in a "deplorable, undignified and unacceptable" manner in December 2006. Then again, while I am still in the Office as British Prime Minister, I warn Robert Mugabe to take notice of this fresh event. Besides, we have been deeply shocked and regret that our civilised troops (British and Americans) have been involved in torture and other inhuman treatment of Iraqi prisoners. We have seen the appalling images from Iraq's Abu Ghraib prison and pitiless killings of innocent Iraqi civilians by the US civilised soldiers (who need now to go ethical training on the ground) that touched and offended the conscience of humankind. Indeed, we have no doubt in our minds that those pictures of Iraqi prisoners deliberately left naked by our international humanitarian liberator soldiers are hugely embarrassing for the White House and Number 10 Downing Street. However, we can assure the entire world that investigations are underway, and justice will be done to those who will be found guilty. Nevertheless, Bush has won the 2004 US election, and I, as a result of following Bush in his illegal war in Iraq, I won our British elections with a reduced majority in Parliament as a protest against that war. Blair will move on to tell Africans the following: concerning Zimbabwe, our position to that African dictator remains resolute. Uncivilised militias and supporters of ZANU-PF have been involved in beating and intimidation of their ZANU-PF opponents; Robert Mugabe has rigged the Zimbabwe 2002 election and this matter will not go away; we do not accept the confirmation by the SADC that the Zimbabwean Parliamentary elections held in Mach 2005, reflected the will of Zimbabwean people or were fair and free; therefore, our decision of removing Robert Mugabe from power is justified because Thabo Mbeki is not acting our way. All this may look like joke, but, this is what African people can learn from Western high moral and rational superiority.

However, let me progress further. Once Blair had delivered his message to Africans, he could not, with any measure of sustainable honesty, maintain that "regime change" (in the world of weaker states) was a new phenomenon or a new form of Western world dominion. Let it be recalled that after the Second World War ended in 1945, and particularly during the period of the Cold War, many regimes/governments around the world had ultimately been changed by the Central Intelligence Agency (CIA), through its different well-sophisticated undercover operations. The history of the CIA is well documented in Latin America, for example, American's defeat in the Bay of Pigs (Cuba) in an attempted operation alongside Cuban rebels to remove the Cuban "socialist revolution" of the Lider Maximo Fidel Raul Castro in 1960; Jacobo Arbenz was ousted in a CIA-organised military coup in Guatemala. In 1954 the CIA prepared a group of Guatemalan exiles under the command of Carlos Acastillo Armas and it funded the training, equipment, and payment of the mercenary troops who launched an invasion of Guatemala. While the CIA had engaged in a vicious propaganda campaign, the US air force bombed the capital of Guatemala and other important cites, forcing Colonel Jacob Arbenz Guzmán to quit office after losing support of his own army. The CIA's operation also included the compilation of lists of individuals it wanted to eliminate, detain or deport from Guatemala after its coup succeeded. This is the reason the young socialist activist Che Guevara had to flee from Guatemala to Mexico where for the first time he met Fidel Castro in exile in 1955; the American downfall and arrest in December 1989 of General Noriega, President of Panama; in Congo/Kinshasa, suspicion had remained in the minds of many African people that the CIA might have been involved in the death of the Congolese Marxist Patrice Lumumba, who briefly held the position of Congolese Prime Minister from 30 June to September 13, 1960. He died in a very sombre manner just days after being dismissed from his position. The suspicion never evaporated in the minds of many Congolese people because the CIA helped the late President Mobutu Sese Seko to oust the late and first Congolese President, Joseph Kasa-Vubu. Mobutu subsequently seized power in the Congo in 1965 and maintained his reign for 32 years despite his dictatorship one-party regime. He owned the gigantic Congo, as King Leopold II of Belgium owned it as his personal possession. The dictator was one of the Cold War rulers in Africa who easily and quickly enriched in exchange for providing the US with the assistance that they required of African allies in the fight against Communist world expansion. As I mentioned earlier, history is learned not only through academic books and lectures, but also through simple recounts, narration and chats. During my stay in the political and security prison of Sao-Paulo in Luanda/Angola between 1982 and 1984, I met with some high-ranking Lumumbist opposition members in exile who were also prisoners there. Interestingly, their accounts on Lumumba and his assassination are of similar information I found in a book called 'The Congo from Leopold to Kabila, a people's history – 2002' – by Georges Nzongola-Ntalaja, a Congolese intellectual with background knowledge of Congo's history. The legislative victory of the Mouvement National Congolais 'MNC' (Congolese National Movement) led by Lumumba with the coalition of Congolese nationalist parties amid the American Cold War imperative posed a serious threat to the Belgian neo-colonialist motivation and, in general, was a threat to Western political and economic ambitions in Central Africa. The prominent and radical nationalist Lumumba was viewed in the West as a serious menace to Western interests and as a bridge for the expansion of communism in central Africa which could extend even further to Southern African region. Therefore, to prevent this happening, a plot masterminded by Americans and Belgians and their manipulated Congolese allies (the so-called Congolese national-ist moderates, including Joseph Désiré Mobutu), culminated first in the sacking by President Joseph Kasa-Vubu of Lumumba as Congolese Prime Minister on September 5, 1960 for allegations of the slaughter of innocent Congolese people of Mbuji-Maji – massacres allegedly conducted by the Armée National Congolese 'ANC' (Congolese National Army), then under the control of the Prime Minister. Lumumba was subsequently detained, and finally assassinated or executed.

Sponsorship and other forms of support to rebel groups have been among some features of the US administrations in changing unwanted regimes/gov-ernments around the world – economic sanctions and embargoes, such as the unsuccessful 40 years' US embargo imposed on Cuba aimed at removing the Socialist revolution of Fidel Castro, also played a part in the US doctrine of "regime change".

However, only one morning after Ben Laden's spectacular massive at-tacks, the world's worst terrorist attacks on the Trade Centre twin towers, Pentagon and a plane crash in Pennsylvania, which made Bush to become a wounded lion and signalled to Americans that the US was vulnerable to enemy penetration, thus, changing the course of Americans normal life in one way or another, the doctrine of "regime change" then came to be used strongly and publicly by the Bush administration. "Regime change" was invoked to remove rogue regimes which have links, support and harbour terrorists. As a result, the Taliban regime in Afghanistan was immediately removed after September 11. And subsequently, although with unsubstan-tiated evidence linking Iraq with September 11 terror and a misleading intelligence about the non-existence of Saddam's WMD, eventually, under the US and the UK's unilateral decision, Saddam Hussein's regime was also finally removed in May 2003, when George Bush himself arrogantly de-clared that major combats in Iraq were over. The President was wrong.

"Regime change" was not invoked in such fashion when the "big man" of the Balkans, the late Slobodan Milosevic (who in March 2006 died in The Hague international criminal prison), was committing his atrocities in the region, particularly during his ethnic cleansing of Albanians in Kosovo. Albeit, it is obvious that Milosevic's main political opponent party had ben-efited from the effect of NATO's bombardment of Yugoslavia and might have received support from the West during the Yugoslavian electoral campaign; however, Slobodan Milosevic was eventually defeated through the polls, not removed through the US doctrine of "regime change".

Even though, the US and the UK have changed the regime in Iraq, Africans did not expect that Blair could explore this American formula to invoke the removal of President Robert Mugabe from office; instead, what the world expected was to see Blair again following Bush to another pre-emptive strike and "regime change" in North Korea, Syria, Libya, and particularly, in Iran, an implacable enemy of the USA – Iran has been regarded as being hostile to the US for many years. The Iran's authorities from top to bottom are aware that the US claims that Iran supports international terrorism. It was claimed that in April 1992, some Iranian citizens or the Iranian Government bombed the Israeli Embassy in Buenos Aires (Argentine); the Iranian Government does not endorse the Arab-Israeli peace negotiations because it gives moral and financial support to the Palestinian group of fundamentalists; the Iranian Government has been accused of training agents to carry out attacks against foreign tourists in the Arab world; accused of providing military means to Hamas to carry out attacks against Israelis; Iran's massive purchase of arms from the former Soviet Union, after the war with Iraq had ended in 1988 became suspicious because it had no legitimate security concerns. From 1989 to 1993, it was reported that Iran had acquired (from the Soviet Union) sophisticated military equipment aimed at deterring and denying other countries access to the sea, weapons such as sub-marines and long-range Soviet military air planes which are sophistically designed to target aircraft carriers. Now that Saddam's regime is finished, Iran's programme to build WMD brought a fever to the US politicians, which still needs a cure. The US administration strongly believes that this time, the main threat to US interests in the region would come from Iran. The dispute between Iran and the International Atomic Energy Agency (IAEA) on Iran's nuclear programme, which has been now referred to UN Security Council, has since been seized by the US as an opportunity to advance her imperialistic agenda – Now there are rumours of a US possible strike on Iran nuclear facilities and the prospects of talks between the US and Iran. But Bush and Blair do not talk with rogue regimes and terrorists, however, now let us wait and see.

Progressing further, many African leaders have been painted as evils and fascist dictators by some ethnocentric British politicians, therefore, it is very important to remind Blair and Western citizens that the sole objective of the Heads of African States and Governments, who met in Accra in 1963, was to establish the unity of Africa by pledging each nation of the African continent to oppose any subversive activities; avoid conduct of hostile propaganda campaigns directed against each other and adopt dialogue with good faith to settle any conflict that may arise between states. Two paragraphs of the convention entitled "African Charter on Human and People's Rights" state:

"CONSIDERING the Charter of the Organisation of African Unity,

which stipulates that 'freedom, equality, justice and dignity are essential objectives for the achievement of the legitimate aspirations of the African peoples".

"CONVINCED that it is henceforth essential to pay a particular attention to the right to development and that civil and political rights cannot be dissociated from economic, social and cultural rights in their conception as well as universality and that the satisfaction of economic, social and cultural rights is a guarantee for the enjoyment of civil and political rights".

This is a confirmation that suggests that this spirit could not have come from the minds of such dictators as the West refers to, but only from those who have compassion and want to see their continent and people united for a better future. But as the world was already divided and influenced by two opposite superpowers, dictating the world order under two rival ideological influences (capitalism and communism) supported by their military supremacy, and forcing African leaders to choose one or other side, with no room to express neutrality, which could come to a cost of their own lives and the removal of their governments. Hence, their initial ideas and the prospect of running the affairs of the continent on African terms sadly did not succeed. Again, in view of mainstream Africans, this African end-goal was an important step undertaken by Africans to move in the direction that was hoped to bring peoples of Africa together, as the European Union has been trying to do for many decades after the Second World War ended. Unfortunately, for African thinkers and intellectuals, that African noble project and the prospects of African countries gaining power and control of their own destinies have been disturbed or impaired by Western imperialistic greed as well as by some powerful nations of the West. Hence, Africans were once again manipulated and divided in the sake of the superpowers' interests in the continent.

"There can be no peace and security in Africa without freedom and political unity". (Kwame Nkrumah)

Another paragraph of the Organisation of African Unity Charter states:

"CONSCIOUS of their duty to achieve the total liberation of Africa, the peoples of which are still struggling for their dignity and genuine independence, and undertaking to eliminate colonialism, neo-colonialism, apartheid, Zionism and dismantle aggressive foreign military bases

and all forms of discrimination, particularly those based on race, ethnic group, colour, sex, language, religion, or political opinions;"

Finally, the persisting British neo-colonialism in Zimbabwe can be perceived simply through the language used within Westminster itself. For instance, after analysing the imperialistic, venomous and rancorous language used in the 15 conclusions and recommendations of the House of Commons Foreign Affairs Committee, Eight Report of Session 2002-2003 on Zimbabwe, on 4 February 2004, I felt compelled to write to the Right Honourable Donald Anderson, Labour MP for Swansea East, Chairman of the House of Commons Foreign Affairs Committee to express my individual criticism of the Report. In my letter to Mr Anderson, I emphasised that the language used in the 15 conclusions and recommendations of the Committee to the Government could not be appreciated by many African leaders. Although it was not my intention to refute the written evidence in the Report, I suggested to him that we ought to remind ourselves of what has now been central to British politics and the consequences of the alleged evidence that took Britain to war in Iraq. I also pointed out that whatever evidence in possession of British politicians, Britain as a former colonial power, should choose its use of language very carefully in dealing with its former colonised countries, and in particular, Zimbabwe. The language used in the Report has been regarded as a vicious, deliberate and inflammable interference in the internal affairs of a sovereign state of Zimbabwe. Just to quote some paragraphs of the Report (7 and 21):

> We conclude that Mugabe's regime may indeed be in its last throes, although we do not underestimate its determination to cling to power…We recommend that a positive decision to provide technical and financial assistance to the independent media in Zimbabwe, in consultation with representatives of those media.

My letter to the Chairman also further emphasised that, far from helping both ZANU-PF (Zimbabwe African National Union-Patriotic Front) and MDC (Movement for Democratic Change) to continue to talk as the South African President Thabo Mbeki and many other African leaders have always suggested, the language found in the conclusions and recommendations elaborated by the House of Commons Foreign Affairs Committee of a former colonial State, indirectly expresses support and encourages the aspirations of the opposition parties in Zimbabwe – whereas, it fuels the existing complicated political crisis in Zimbabwe. To sustain this, let us assess the question that was put to Mr Langworth, former British High Commissioner to Zimbabwe by the committee:

"Is there anything specifically the British Government should be doing to strengthen the opposition forces in Zimbabwe?"

Mr Longworth wisely replied:

No, I think that it would be unwise for the British Government to interfere in any way in the domestic policies of Zimbabwe. I think that on the one hand it is a country that needs to resolve its own politics; we need to make it clear that the framework within which we are prepared to work with the next government is set by human rights rules, good economic management rules and all that, but I think for us to give direct support to a party would be wrong on our part and certainly would do no great help to the cause of the party. I think one of the great difficulties the MDC has had has been the allegations which have been spread by the government media and government spokesmen that in fact the MDC was some kind of front for white farmers and the British government....

See a letter from Steve Priestley, Clerk of Foreign Affairs Committee on behalf of Donald Anderson in the following paragraph.

It should be remembered that throughout the world history, the southern African region has been known to be the only part of the world which has experienced the inhumane and atrocious Western colonial domination. From 1575, Angola was deeply penetrated by Portugal, a relatively a poor European country in European terms – a country which had no resources and any industrial base to develop its large colonial countries around the world. Colonial racism, injustice, oppression, forced labour, arbitrary imprisonment and torture and the improvement of standards of living in Portugal at the expense of black African populations fuelled the nationalist protest that eventually led to a bitterness colonial liberation struggle and confused departure of Portuguese colonists from Angola in November 1975; Mozambique has also endured the Portuguese colonial oppression as Angola did, resulting in fierce liberation struggle that forced Portuguese colonists to depart from the country in June 1975; it was in Namibia (formerly known as South West Africa) that the international trusteeship of a mandated territory culminated to a complicated last decolonisation in Africa. Southern Africa is part of the world where Zimbabwe experienced a white minority rule. Ian Smith hijacked independence through a Unilateral Declaration of Independence (UDI) from a powerful United Kingdom; the white minority regime that committed terror, atrocities and massacre of black African populations with connivance of the civilised West. This part of the world was where an aggressive and political system of apartheid first emerged and finally defeated in South Africa. Peoples of this part of the world have known nothing but gross abuses of their fundamental human rights even when the famous 'Universal Declaration of Human Rights' came into effect in 1948. This part of the Globe is where by proxy Africans fought fiercely each others the two superpowers ideological war, the 'Cold War'   and the part of the Globe that still suffering from enormous effects of the devastation of that West-Soviet ideological war. Some few examples of this are: Western sale of millions landmines which were planted in the region; the destruction of regional infrastructures and the development of thousands of displaced people and refugees across the region during the Cold War. In that same region, white Europeans did not pay compensation to Africans they dispossessed of their land; European farms in Zimbabwe, whether large or small, just dominated agricultural production since white settlers dispossessed Africans of their land in the beginning of 1900; European settlers continue to subjugate Black Africans/Zimbabwean workers by making them cheap labour force in their farms as in the past when they acquired large Zimbabwe's fertile land free of charge.

CHAPTER TWO

TWO

WHY ARE BRITISH MPs FURIOUS AT PRESIDENTS MUGABE AND MBEKI?

We want "regime change" in Zimbabwe. (Tony Blair)
We will "resist regime" change in Zimbabwe. (Thabo Mbeki)
We must not go that way again. (Robert Mugabe)

A Prime Minister from a former colonial state, Mr. Tony Blair, has made the first statement. It is a statement that is not welcomed in Africa and has created a culture of strong circumspection, distrust and fear among those African leaders unwelcome to Westminster and White House, particularly those in Southern region of Africa.

The second statement has been made by a veteran African revolutionary fighter and President of South Africa, Mr Thabo Mvuyelwa Mbeki – a statement viewed at Westminster as being supportive to Mugabe and that has made him the proverbial "unwelcome guest at Westminster". Put it another way, 'a persona non grata'.

The third has been an even 'kick in the teeth' statement made by a veteran African revolutionary fighter and President of Zimbabwe, Mr Robert Gabriel Mugabe, a comrade of Thabo Mbeki, but an implacable African enemy of Tony Blair and many others at Westminster.

From my experience of Africa, the broadly held view of most African leaders has been the imperative endorsement that Africa's problems can be resolved within African terms; thus, rejecting any outside African interference in the internal affairs of sovereign weaker nations of the continent, as the European Union itself rejects the USA's interference in its continental affairs. African leaders may disagree or diverge in many ways, but they always try to preserve their unified position and solidarity when it comes to resist anything they perceive to have an imperialistic and neo-colonialist motive. They are all confident and proud of their principles, and they are right because in 2005 the AU has proved this African approach by rejecting the US/UK calls to intervene in Zimbabwe's Government domestic policy of 'Operation Restore Order' against informal traders, and the 'Operation 'Murambatsvina' (Operation Clear Away the Trash or grime, rubbish, filth). This African solidarity is not accidental, but built out of a long and common colonial struggle that has also been demonstrated in a particular way by the President of Uganda, Mr Yoweri Museveni, during his recent official visit to Zimbabwe, when he made it clear that: *"None outside Africa can demonise Robert Mugabe."*

However, for the vast majority of Africans, particularly for their political leaders, the following is one that surpasses all above statements:

> ***"I believe that, left to ourselves, we can achieve unity on the African continent".*** (Julius Nyerere)

At the outset I want to make it clear that I mention the above statements not because I want to blindly support the stance taken by both Presidents Mugabe and Mbeki. Although I do not dare to rule out human rights concerns in Zimbabwe and, while not allowing myself to be perceived as an interfering foreigner in Zimbabwe's domestic affairs, I will not attempt to refute the statements made by both African leaders. I do not appreciate anti-Mugabe campaign of vilification which does not first recognise that President Mugabe has been a recognisable great leader in Africa and a revolutionary liberator not only of Zimbabwean people, but of African people as a whole from a European dehumanising colonialism – his role in the liberation of South Africans from apartheid is remarkable and offers him honourable place in the history of Africa. Yet again, while I will not allow myself to be regarded as ignorant of ordinary African people's suffering, and the violation of human rights, bad governance, corruption, and so forth, I will not endorse any Western distorted and harmful representations about Africa's problems or any imperialist and interventionist policies that press President Mbeki to play an imperialist role or a dangerous role of policing African sovereign countries on behalf of the UK and the US governments. This book is not a place to endorse neither those at Number 10 and Westminster who do not take a considered look at the Africa's crucial problems and their causes and how they can be resolved nor those who assume to know all the answers to Africa's problems than Africans themselves. It is not a place to appease those immoral, charlatan and dogmatic British MPs/politicians who want to lead not only the British society, but the world by policing, spying and telling other people, particularly people in the so-called Third World what to do, how to behave, how to run their internal affairs, and so forth.

IS KATE HOEY A BRITISH MP OR UNDERCOVER JOURNALIST IN AFRICA? – WAS HER UNDERCOVER MISSION IN ZIMBABWE AUTHORISED BY LABOUR GOVERNMENT AND FUNDED BY BRITISH TAXPAYERS?

Before I publish some extracts from responses received from some British MPs and other officials on Zimbabwe and other world affairs and make some further comments on the subject, I would prefer to first publish some relevant paragraphs in my five-page letter of individual protest to Kate Hoey, British politician and Labour MP for Vauxhall.

My letter to Kate Hoey expressed many true sentiments that I have addressed to many other British MPs too. As it is evident, the British MPs/politicians' long consensus and the broad-based commitment are to see President Mugabe out of power. Hence, Kate travelled to Harare, Zimbabwe, during summer 2005 as a British undercover journalist to secretly film what was happening during the Zimbabwean Government policy of '**Operation Restore Order**' against informal traders, and the '**Operation Murambatsvina**' (Operation Clear Away the Trash or grime, rubbish, filth), conducted between 18 May and early July 2005. She has vehemently protested and reproached the Zimbabwean Government domestic policy. Many Zimbabwean Government officials insist that the policy appears only to the West as being naïve, but in fact, a productive policy in long term. Her imperialist language of "firm action" against President Mugabe only suggests that she has been furious at President Mugabe and strongly condemns President Mbeki for his 'quite diplomacy' and inaction or blind eye to the domestic policies of his neighbouring Zimbabwe. She has even insisted that President Mbeki be barred from 2005 G8 – a ridiculous and disdainful approach to Africans.

Officially, the Government of Zimbabwe on 18 May, 2005, launched a domestic policy '**Operation Murambatsvina**' **(Restore Order)** aimed at dealing with crime, squalor, and lawlessness, and rebuild and reorganize urban settlements and small and medium enterprises (SMEs) in a way that would bring dignity, order and prosperity to the stakeholders and the nation at large. According to Government official document, the operation was a follow-up to the anti-corruption campaign started by Government in early 2004 to cleanse the financial services sector, which had become the centre of speculative activities. It is important to remember that similar to Zimbabwean Government initiative that leads to demolition of shanty towns has been taking place in Africa and elsewhere, and it is also similar to the demolition in large extent that has been happening in China, where people have been left homeless. But China, as giant nation and the 21st-century world fast growing economic power, its President has not been banned from travelling to Europe Union and US. The Zimbabwean Government policy **'Operation Murambatsvina'** was what prompted a British politician/MP, a compassionate British woman from a former colonial state to undertake an illegal and spying mission in Zimbabwe. On her arrival back to Britain, she rushed to the TV and Internet to make British public base their judgement and conclusion on her well selected video images that she brought from Zimbabwe. Undoubtedly, no African MP would be interested to come to Western Europe to secretly film those people who sleep rough on streets of London and eat from bins.

Nevertheless, following the report of the UN Secretary General's Special Envoy, Mrs Anna Kajumulo of 21 July 2005, in its preliminary response to the report, the Government of Zimbabwe has briefly concluded the following: (Also see response by Government of Zimbabwe to the report by the UN special envoy on Operation Murambatsvina/Restore Order published in July 2005)

3.6.15　The Government of Zimbabwe will continue to exercise its legitimate responsibility to implement its national laws, including municipal by-laws with the support of the majority of ordinary Zimbabweans. This responsibility is being exercised in the context of the socio-economic policies of Government whose overall objectives and goals are to uplift the lives of ordinary Zimbabweans, in the face of illegal sanctions and unwarranted vilification by Britain and its allies, adversities which the report does not seem too keen to acknowledge.

3.6.16　In its analysis of the situation in Zimbabwe the Report clearly takes-sides with the UK, the US, the white Commonwealth, the EU, as well as the opposition MDC and some sections of civil society who, in pursuit of other agendas, have taken the negative stance of condemning anything and everything done by the Government of Zimbabwe. It is unfortunate that the mission is now being hijacked by some Western countries as an opportunity to intervene in the internal affairs of Zimbabwe. In this regard the government of Zimbabwe deplores the attempts by Tony Blair and his Government to hijack and politicize the UNSE's mission as demonstrated by Blair's exhortation at the start of the fact-finding mission that the UNSE should come up with a "good report" that he would take to the Security Council.

3.6.17 The Government of Zimbabwe notes the suggested entry points by-
international players that have been made in the spirit of mutual cooperation and assistance. The suggested entry points will have to be agreed
upon with due regard to Zimbabwe's sovereignty, national laws and development priorities.

One might already argue that if an investigation is allowed over British
genuineness concerns about land reform policy introduced by the Government
of Zimbabwe, it would find that some of hardliner and aggressive British
politicians who press for "robust action – resolute action" and draconian approach to ZANU-PF and its President, would have in one way or another,
sombre interests in Zimbabwe; would have settler families, relatives or friends
occupying Africa's fertile lands, particularly lands in southern Africa.

Kate Hoey brought to the UK those images of **'Operation Murambatsvina'** to also help her campaign against the deportation of Zimbabwean
asylum seekers by British immigration. This is a step too far which is intended
to inflame the internal situation and divide the nation of Zimbabwe in the
sake of British economic and strategic interests as the case of actual Iraq. It is
not a matter for reticent politicians such as Hoey to campaign, instead, given
the historical connection between both countries, in which many thousands
of British stock still feel comfortable to live in Zimbabwe; and taking into
consideration the huge wealth that the UK had made out of Zimbabwe's fertile land at the expense of downtrodden black Zimbabwean workers, today,
Zimbabwean people would deserve to be treated generously and faithfully
welcomed by British people. Zimbabweans do not arrive here in mass groups;
Zimbabweans are not the ones who come to the UK to try to influence or
alter the way British people live; Zimbabweans have been known as peaceful
people; they do not pose any kind of threat to the British national security.
Therefore, while Zimbabwean asylum seekers await for their immigration decisions to be made on the basis of individual merit as a single principle for all
asylum seekers, they do not deserve to be locked up in the British immigration detention centres because they have sought refuge in the UK. If regular
deportation of those who are unwanted in this country is needed to regulate
the current chaotic immigration situation, then, Zimbabweans should appear
at the bottom of the list for this regular deportation.

African people also should know that some Western politicians and celebrities are volunteering to go round Africa simply to take some emotional
pictures with those poor faces of African women and children so that they
can come back home and make some noises on their national TV screens and

papers just to expand their fame.

However, the Right Honourable Kate Hoey neither replied nor acknowledged my letter.

Another compelling reason for publishing extracts from letters I received from many British MPs is due to the fact that some MPs have just invoked ministerial and constituency commitments or parliamentary convention, a restriction which prevents them from entering into correspondence with me on the issues I have raised with them. In receiving replies from many other MPs on the same issues I have raised, I wonder if Parliamentary convention applies to some and not to others, though there are heavyweight, middleweight and lightweight MPs in the House of Commons.

1. The following are some relevant extracts from my five-page letter to Kate Hoey:

Rt. Hon. Kate Hoey, MP for Vauxhall
House of Commons
London SW1A 0AA

29 June 2005

Dear Kate Hoey,

I am Mr. Zimi Roberto, an African citizen from Angola, and I have been living in the United Kingdom since 1989.

I have carefully followed your recent comments on Zimbabwe and your vicious accusations made against President Robert Mugabe quite everywhere, in the newspapers, TV, in the debates at House of Commons. As an African citizen from Angola, I really felt compelled to write to you to express my deepest indignation with regard to your imperialistic endeavour in Africa. This is to say that as an MP of a former colonial ruler, from thousands of miles from Zimbabwe, your job is not meant to undertake [undercover] dangerous activities of secretly filming what you perceive or judge to be bad in Zimbabwe. I can assure you that no African MP would be interested in doing that in Africa, in Europe or elsewhere in the world.

I regret the fact that in your biography, I found that Angola, my

country, has been among your countries of interest in the world (Angola, Bosnia, Oman and Zimbabwe). I suggest that you stay aloof from Angola's internal affairs, because Angolan people have moved further to a direction of national reconciliation and peaceful solutions in their political affairs. We reject any western interference.

I completely disagree with your prescribed British foreign policy towards a sovereign African state of Zimbabwe. It is, I must say, regrettable and a dangerous British foreign policy in attempting to influence President Thabo Mbeki to press for political changes in Zimbabwe or in any other African country. Apart of Africa, do you do that somewhere else in the world? Who are you to tell a veteran African politician such as President Thabo Mbeki what to do with Zimbabwe - Is President Mbeki's role in Africa to takeover African countries' domestic policies? Your insistence for President Mbeki be barred from G8 is just ridiculous and a disdain approach to [for] Africans.

While many British politicians as yourself have been reticent about the root causes of the bitterness or contentious [relations] between the UK and Zimbabwe, they have been trying to explore in Zimbabwe anything whatever minor to blow it out of proportion to the British public. Land has been central to the contentious [relations] between the two sovereign states, Britain and Zimbabwe - and we cannot discuss the political and economic crises in Zimbabwe without referring first to the 1979 Lancaster House Agreement, the constitutional arrangement that led Zimbabwe to Independence in 1980. Democracy and human rights came after as a post Cold War newest western weapon to undermine those Africans leaders who do not comply with the US/UK wishes - a vicious pretext used by some British politicians at No 10 Downing Street and Westminster to protect British economic interests in Zimbabwe, and eventually, pave the way to topple President Mugabe's Government through a British military intervention, thus turning Zimbabwe into Africa's Iraq.

Let me recall to you that the South African President Thabo Mbeki has been blaming Britain and other western powers for causing land crisis in Zimbabwe. Thus, for many occasions, he insistently stated publicly that:

> *"... Britain and other western countries had broken* *promises, dating from 1979, to fund peaceful land redis-* *tribution in Zimbabwe... ".* **Therefore, can you answer** **this question: Is President Thabo Mbeki's statement a** **fabrication? Is he a liar too?**

In addition, on democracy and human rights, President Mbeki also states:

> *"Those who fought for a democratic Zimbabwe, with* *thousands paying the supreme price during the struggle,* *and forgave their oppressors and tortures in a spirit of* *national reconciliation, have turned into repugnant* *enemies of democracy. [yet] those who, in the interest* *of their 'kith and kin', did what they could to deny the* *people of Zimbabwe their liberty, for as long as they* *could, have become the eminent defenders of the demo-* *cratic rights of the people of Zimbabwe. We will resist* *this upside-down view of Africa".*

Following the Commonwealth Heads of Government Meeting (CHOGM) in Abuja, Nigeria, between December 5 and 8 2003, in his weekly electronic letter in his party's website journal, ANC Today, President Mbeki emphasized:

> *"...Britain opposed Zimbabwe's readmission to the* *Commonwealth this week merely to protect its "white* *settler, colonial kith and kin". And that western are* *using the demand for Mugabe to respect human rights* *merely as a tool for "regime change" in Zimbabwe".*

Moreover, it would be unwise for a British MP like you to expose President Robert Mugabe to the British public as a foolish African old man, who woke up one morning and ordered his ZANU-FP supporters to go out and violently repossess from white settler farmers their land inherited from their forefathers - again, it would be unwise to British public to believe that an African revolution-ary liberator, who has spent 10 years in a white colonial prison, spent many years of his best life time fighting for the liberation of his people from an appalling human conditions under colonialism, would not hesitate to turn his guns against the very same people [whose] he has fought for without any reason whatsoever.

If your compassion for human rights of the people of Zimbabwe was genuine, you would have recommended to your Government to go quite everywhere in the world and change all unwanted undemocratic and despotic regimes - it would go first to Burma to free **Aung San Suu Kyi, Burmese human rights activist and political leader who has been under house arrest for so many years** - change regime in China in favour of those Chinese [students] perished during Tasmanian Square massacres in 1999 - change regimes in Russia, Cuba, North Korea, Georgia - and finally, by now, Britain would have closed the American Guantanamo Bay Prison, which has become a very bad **ICON** for a country that has claimed to be a vanguard and champion of spreading the values of freedom, human rights and democracy around the world...

Your firm action against President Mugabe suggests a British military intervention in Zimbabwe, as many politicians at No 10 Downing Street and Westminster envisage. Let me bring [back to] your memory Africa's recent history. In 1994, the world saw more than half million African people, including innocent children, women and old people who perished in Rwanda's tribal conflict. You, the British woman with such compassion for Africans' suffering did not press for a British military intervention to stop that remarkable world tragedy in Rwanda. Now, are you pressing for British military invasion of Zimbabwe because of the demolition which has left according to your own figure, a quarter of million people homeless? - are you the UN [with] the legitimacy of overtaking Zimbabwe's Government domestic policies? Have you told the British people who is inviting the UK to change regime in Zimbabwe? Do you understand why the US/UK call for African Union to intervene in Zimbabwe has been rejected by African leaders? Do not you understand that allowing Tony Blair from a former colonial state, from thousands of miles from Zimbabwe to change the current Government of Zimbabwe is tantamount to allowing the return of colonialism to the black continent?

I do not dare to interfere in the political affairs of Zimbabwe, however, it is not kind to see those recent well selected images you brought from Zimbabwe with regard to 'Operation Drive Out Trash', which many of you regard as aimed at punishing [out] opposition supporters by President Mugabe. To me, it is obvious that President Mugabe would not wait or take the risk of punishing those Zimbabweans who did not vote for his party, after wining with a landslide victory in the recent Parliamentary elections held last Mach, that you and many British politicians do not recognise to be free and fair. Britain as Zimbabwe's former coloniser state, accused of neo-colonial propaganda and vicious policies to undermine ZANU-PF and its leader, would perhaps, refrain to be the first to believe and support what has been said against Zimbabwean's Government…

Yours sincerely

Zimi Roberto

Cc: anyone

2. In respect to the contents in the above letter sent to Hoey (a copy sent to Mr Richard Benyon, Conservative MP for Newbury), and also in another letter questioning him whether it is true or false the statement made by President Thabo Mbeki that ***"Britain and other Western countries had broken promises, dating from 1979, to fund peaceful land redistribution".*** The following is the disingenuous and harsh reaction by Mr Richard Benyon, on his replying letter to me on 11 July 2005:

Dear Mr Roberto

Thank you for writing to me concerning Zimbabwe. I firmly support Kate Hoey's bravery in visiting Zimbabwe to expose the evils of the Mugabe regime. I am actively involved in bringing justice to Zimbabwe.

I am disgusted by the inability of African leaders including Thabo Mbeki to condemn Mugabe and his coterie of gangsters who have brought such misery to Zimbabwe.

I skimmed through your daft letter to Kate Hoey for whom I have the highest respect, and see that you are trotting out the tired old accusation of imperial intentions of anyone who raises concerns about Zimbabwe. I am sure if you gave the issue a moment's thought you would realise how ridiculous such an accusation

sounds. I suggest you go to Zimbabwe in the same way that Kate
Hoey did and judge for yourself what kind of ruler it has.

Richard Benyon.

Further to this, being incompetent to grasp my independent views
and opinions – unable to argue and maintain his unsubstantiated views on
Zimbabwe, Benyon chooses the approach of attacking and silencing those
who use the freedom of expression to expose the deliberate Westminster's
misrepresentation of Africa. Benyon went on beyond to digress from the real
subject and consider my views as being of racist nature. The following are my
last two letters to Benyon that have infuriated him:

a) Mr Richard Benyon, Con MP for Newbury

09 August 2005

Dear Mr. Benyon,

As one of the genuine British champions of world justice and human rights, I am certain that you have been following the current
news/documentary on the most sickest and shocking images of
children's conditions in one of the Philippines' prisons - images that
offend humankind conscience.

I had been in the Angolan highest security prisons of Estrada de
Catete and Sao Paulo in Luanda for 2 years (1982-84), together
with British mercenaries made prisoners of war by Marxist MPLA
Government in 1976 and all released in January 1984. I can assure
you that I had not seen anything there to compare with the scene
were [we] are seeing in Philippines' prison.

I am sure if you could faithfully give the situation in Philippines a
moment's thought, you would conclude that your justice or British
invasion or regime change is not primarily needed in Zimbabwe,
but somewhere else.

Yours sincerely

Zimi Roberto

b) Mr Richard Benyon, British politician/Con MP for Newbury

House of Commons
London SW1 A OAA

06 September 2005

Dear Mr Benyon,

Further to my individual protest against Western interference in
the affairs of African sovereign nations, this time, I would like you
to draw a simple comparison between the neglect which resulted
to the perishing of thousands of lives, mostly lives of poor black
people in the wealthiest nation in the world, the USA and the minor societal incidents in the African state of Zimbabwe. As you are
well aware, many reliable reports confirm that after the September
11th terrorist attacks on the USA, Bush started to cut largely the
federal funding sought to build strong protection for New Orleans
and its population from a predicted disastrous storms. More than
half of fund cutting has been then diverted to war against terrorism
and his pre-planned unpopular and illegal war in Iraq with the sole
objective of removing Saddam Hussein. The current domestic policies of arrogant Bush and his administration and slow response to
the most horrible storm in the history of the USA are largely to be
blamed for the scale of the disaster, the suffering of affected people,
overwhelmingly poor black people and the death tall of Katrina
hurricane in the evacuated city of New Orleans. What is currently
happening in that part of the world is utterly unacceptable and
many people already regard it as crime against humanity for the
fact that the US government possesses all the means that could
minimise the impact of that predicted natural disaster, and move
quickly in saving lives after the storm. This situation raises serious
questions - and someone must be hold responsible. I understand
that your passion is to see justice for the ordinary and poor black
people of Zimbabwe. However, right now, people are still dying
in New Orleans, and I would definitely except you to rush to the
House of Commons to discuss about those black people affected
by disastrous Bush's domestic policies and press the Government
for a United Nations immediate action, as it was the case with
Zimbabwean Government policy of urban renewal campaign aimed
at maintaining a long term standards of health of its people.

Finally, after more than a week of appalling, shocking and disgusting images from New Orleans, I have not yet seen any British politician on any British TV channel or newspaper taking the courage to expose the failure of Bush's administration as many of you promptly do with regard to Governments in Africa, particularly with regard to the current detested Government in Zimbabwe. Let us leave it to the history.

Zimi Roberto

Cc: Anyone

The latter has been the letter that has irritated the Conservative MP, Mr Richard Benyon. The above letter has been returned to me with Benyon's handwriting note at the top of it, which read:

You seem happy to condemn millions of black people to misery at the hands of fascist dictators like Mugabe. You are therefore not someone with whom there is any point in taking seriously. Take your unpleasant racist views to some other MP [MPs].

Being branded racist because of exposing the truth through free expression is not pleasant to anybody. Therefore, to express my dissatisfaction over Benyon's political immaturity and seek further information on how to submit a formal complaint to his party, on 12 October, I wrote to the Conservative Chairman, Rt Hon Francis Maude. His slapping in my face replying letter was as following:

Mr Zimi Roberto
8 Brindley House
Alfred Road
London W2 5EY

17th October 2005

Dear Mr Roberto

Thank you for your letter dated 12th October 2005.

There is no formal mechanism with which you can complain about the conduct of an MP other than by not voting for him or her at the next General Election.

Yours sincerely

The Rt Hon Francis Maude MP
Chairman of The Conservative Party
CC Richard Benyon MP".

Moreover, the following are relevant extracts from responses from some British MPs and other officials on the questions whether it is true or false the statement made by President Thabo Mbeki that *"Britain and other Western countries had broken promises, dating from 1979, to fund peaceful land redistribution"* and question on other British foreign policies:

3. From Melissa Chowdhury and Miss ELEESHA SMITH, 10 Downing Street, Direct Communication Unit, on behalf of the Prime Minister:

10 DOWNING STREET
LONDON SW1A 2AA

From the Direct Communication Unit 3 February 2004
Mr Zimi Roberto
8 Brindley House
Alfred Road
London
W2 5EY

Dear Mr Roberto

The Prime Minister has asked me to thank you for your recent letter.

He was pleased that you felt able to write and has asked that a careful note be made of your comments.

Additionally, he has asked that your letter be passed to the Foreign and Commonwealth Office who have responsibility for this subject so that they, too, are aware of your concerns and can send you any comments they may have direct.

Yours sincerely

MELISSA CHOWDHURY

5 March 2004

Dear Mr Roberto

Mr Blair receives many thousands of letters each week. He would like to reply to all letters personally, however, as I am sure you will appreciate his many other duties makes this impossible.

Mr Blair appreciates the time that people take to write to him, but, he must delegate to his staff and Government Departments the responsibility for dealing with many of hem. It was for this reason that your letter was forwarded to the Department concerned [FCO].

Yours sincerely

MISS ELEESHA SMITH

4. From the Right Honourable Clare Short, Labour MP for Birmingham Ladywood (26 January 2004):

                          from The Rt Ron Clare Short MP

Dear Zimi Roberto

Thank you for your letter. I agree with much that you say though I believe President Mbeki is making mistakes over Zimbabwe and that the suffering of the people of Zimbabwe is very serious.

However, as I am no longer a member of the UK Government I suggest that you consider sending your letter to my successor, Hilary Benn, at the Department for International Development, or to Chris Mullin who is the minister for Africa in the Foreign and Commonwealth Office.

Best wishes

Yours sincerely

Clare Short.

5. Late Right Honourable Robin Cook, Labour MP for Livingston:

No reply to my letter of 19 January 2004 – is it a Parliamentary convention?

6. From the Right Honourable Alan Beith, Liberal Democrats MP for Berwick (22 January 2004):

Dear Mr. Roberto,

Thank you for your letter about the problems affecting Africa and British foreign policy in Africa

I have passed your letter on to the Liberal Democrats Shadow Foreign Secretary, Rt. Hon. Sir Menzies Campbell, MP., for his information.

7. From Richard Chapman on behalf of Paul Boateng, Labour MP for Brent South (17 March 2004):

Dear Mr Roberto,

Thank you for your letter of January 19th to Mr Boateng regarding African policy, Zimbabwe, human rights and related issues.

Mr Boateng thanks you for taking the time to write to him with your thoughts, and at such length, but unfortunately his ministerial and constituency commitments mean he is prevented from entering into a correspondence with you on the issues you have raised.

Your comments have all been noted though and he is grateful for your sharing them with him.

In accordance with the parliamentary convention, I am also copying this letter to your own MP, Karen Buck.

Richard Chapman
Office Manager for Rt Hon Paul Boateng MP
CC: Karen Buck MP.

8. From Mr. David Lamy, Lab MP for Tottenham - January 2004:

Only a House of Commons' acknowledgement card was received.

9. From Mr. Andrew Hopkinson at Southern Africa Department of Foreign

and Common Office on behalf of Chris Mullin, Minister for Africa (02
Feb and 03 Mar 2004):

Dear Mr Roberto

Thank you for your letter of 19 January to Chris Mullin, Minister
for Africa. I have been asked to reply.

You mention President Mbeki's claim that the situation in
Zimbabwe has been caused by the UK and Western powers. The
current crisis in Zimbabwe is due to ZANU (PF)'s disastrous policies which have led to inflation of almost 600 per cent and unemployment of over 70%. In addition, it is estimated that six million
people (over half the population) will need food aid during the
January to April pre- harvest period. Rather than being the cause
of the crisis, the UK is helping the people of Zimbabwe. Since
September 2001 we have provided £62 million in aid; £20 million
in the current financial year alone. Over the coming months we will
be providing further humanitarian aid. Hardly the actions of a government which merely wishes to protect its white settler, colonial
kith and kin.

Thank you for your further letter of 4 February to Mr Mullin. I
have also been asked to reply to this letter.

You ask about the underlying causes of the crisis in Zimbabwe.
The cause of the current crisis lies in the disastrous policies of the
ZANU (PF) regime. The "fast track" programme for land redistribution has had a devastating impact on commercial farming
and has resulted in many Zimbabwean farm workers loosing their
homes and jobs. Bad economic policies have ensured that foreign
direct investment has almost dried up and assistance from international financial institutions, such as the IMF and World Bank, has
stopped.

We recognise that South Africa has a role to play in helping to find
a solution to the current crisis in Zimbabwe. We welcome President
Mbeki's continued engagement.

Andrew Hopkinson
Africa Department (Southern).

10. From Steve Priestley, Clerk of Foreign Affairs Committee on behalf of Donald Anderson, British Labour MP for Swansea East and Chairman of Foreign Affairs Committee (09 February 2004):

Dear Zimi Roberto,

I am sure he [Donald Anderson] shares your sentiments about the need for greater understanding between our continents and of the mutual benefit which can be derived from that, but you should not expect the Committee to shrink from speaking out against abuses of human rights in Zimbabwe just as it has spoken out against the detention by the USA of people without trial at Guantanamo Bay, and against other abuses around the globe, wherever they occur.

Steve Priestey
Clerk of the Committee.

11. From the Right Honourable Michael Ancram, Conservative MP for Devizes and the then Shadow Foreign Secretary (07 September 2004):

Dear Mr Roberto, Conservative

Thank you for your letter of 30 August regarding your concerns about what you term *"the British aggressive foreign policy towards the world weakest nations, particularly the British vicious policy towards Zimbabwe"*.

I read your letter with care and have noted the points you make, however I am afraid I cannot share your analysis of the situation in Zimbabwe. Zimbabwe was, for many years, the breadbasket of Africa producing enough food not simply to feed itself but to feed much of the continent. That its own people are now on the brink of starvation and refugees are what today flow to its neighbours is down to the policy that has been pursued by Robert Mugabe.

He has demonstrated contempt for the rule of law with his regime being responsible for murder and violence. The way in which he has pursued land reform with illegal land grabs, with established farmers replaced by regime loyalists, has led to a complete collapse of Zimbabwe's agricultural base. Land lies idle, machinery is unused and instead of seeking to feed his people and hold free and fair elections to give them a voice I believe that Mr Mugabe persists in trying to invoke a non- existent neo-colonialist plot against him as a reason for the state of his country. I am sorry that you do not agree with my view on this matter, but hope that you will respect the strength of my opinion as I respect yours".

"Rt Hon Michael Ancram QC MP.

12. From Mr. Vernon Coaker, Labour MP for Gelding:

Only a House of Commons' acknowledgement card was received.

The following are the responses to my letters of 01 and 05 July 2005:

13. Right Honourable David Blunkett, Labour MP- Secretary of State, Department for Work and Pensions (11 July 2005):

Dear Zimi

Thank you very much for your long and interesting letter.

I am afraid (and I am writing immediately post the terrorist attack on London). I am not able to give you a detailed reply.

I do however take the view that we have a responsibility to each other and that is including one nation to another.

I wish for instance that the world had intervened to stop the genocide in Rwanda eleven years ago - I hope we will have courage to support all those who are prepared to bring democracy to down trodden people who are exploited by those who consume the wealth of a great continent.

With very best wishes,

Rt Hon David Blunkett MP.

14. Right Honourable Nick Brown, Labour MP for Newcastle Upon Tyne East and Wallsend :

No reply has been received yet – is it a Parliamentary convention?

15. Mr. David Winnick, Labour MP for Walsall North:

No reply has been received yet – is it a Parliamentary convention?

16. Rt. Hon. Frank Dobson, Labour MP for Holborn (06 July 2005):

Dear Zimi Roberto,

I acknowledge receipt of your letter dated 1 July.

In line with Parliamentary convention, I have today forwarded your letter to your own Member of Parliament, Karen Buck (Regent's Park and Kensington North Constituency). However, in acknowledging receipt of your letter, I would ask you to let me know from where you gained the impression that I have no interest in Africa. This, quite simply, is not true.

Yours sincerely,

cc Karen Buck MP.

17. From Miss Anne McIntosh, Conservative MP for Vale of York (05 July 2005):

Dear Mr Roberto

Thank you for your letter, dated 1 July, regarding the present Zimbabwean regime and international pressure on Robert Mugabe to respect democratic freedoms and human rights.

With regards to Zimbabwe, I must first challenge your claim that President Mugabe is a democratically elected leader. A number of international organisations contested the validity of the recent election results in which opposition supporters were intimidated, attacked and prevented from voting.

The interest now being shown in Zimbabwe is a direct result of Mugabe's absolute disregard for the rule of law and lack of respect for any human rights. His latest attempts to control political opponents and their supporters through his 'operation lean-up' have created more than one million homeless Zimbabweans, solely with the intention of driving these people into the countryside, where he is able to control their access to food. Whatever view one takes of international interest in Africa, one cannot deny the blatant disregard for individual freedom shown by President Mugabe.

"However, whilst I welcome the impact of recent events such Live
8, and recognise the importance of the forthcoming G8 summit, I
truly believe that any change has to [be] brought about by African
nations. The African Union has a major role to play in encouraging
nations to respect democracy and respect human rights. As such,
I am disappointed by the lack of any condemnation for President
Mugabe by the South African President Thabo Mbeki, who could
place great political pressure on the Zimbabwean leader.

I hope that this gives you an idea of my feelings on this most
important matter. I can assure you that I am not supporting an
imperialist policy in Africa, but feel that people everywhere should
be able to live in freedom without fear of persecution.

Miss Anne McIntosh LLB MP
Member of Parliament for the Vale of York
Shadow Minister for Foreign Affairs.

Interestingly, Miss Ana McIntosh has subsequently taken a great deal of
her time to write to me a five page-long letter on her understanding of the
contention between the UK and Zimbabwe. She also spent much time talk-
ing about £62 millions from British Governments to assist with land redistribution in Zimbabwe - small £millions that the Bush administration has made
available to reward people with reliable information leading to the capture of
most wanted terrorists - $25 millions were put on Saddam's head, $15 millions were put on each Saddam Hussein's sons heads, Uday and Quasay, $25
and $15 millions have already been available for the heads of Bin Laden and
Zaqarwi respectively.

18. From Dr Jenny Tonge, former Liberal Democrats MP for Richmond
Park:

No longer LD MP, but acknowledgement letter was received.

19. From the Right Honourable Sue Doughty, Liberal Democrats MP for
Guilford (06 July 2005):

Dear Mr. Roberto

Thank you for your letter and good wishes. Unfortunately I was narrowly defeated at the General Election on the 5th May this year and consequently am no longer the Member of Parliament for Guildford.

I hope that your interests in British politics, human rights and African development continue and wish you well for the future.

Sue Doughty.

20. From Mr. Michael Fabricant Esq. Conservative MP for Lichfield (11 July 2005):

Dear Mr Roberto

Thank you for your letter of 1st July concerning Africa.

There is a strict rule in Parliament that Members may only deal with matters raised by their own constituents so I am cannot take these issues further on your behalf.

You will appreciate that I have a hectic diary and a heavy constituency postbag. I very much regret, therefore, that I am unable to spend the time needed to give a considered response to your thoughtful letter.

I am sorry about this, but do hope that you will understand.

21. From Ian Philps on behalf of Rt. Hon. Michael Howard, Conservative Leader and MP for Folkestone and Hythe (14 July 2005):

Dear Mr Roberto,

Thank you for your letter to Michael Howard. He has asked me to reply to you on his behalf.

It was kind of you to write. Mr Howard attaches considerable importance to the views that are put to him and your comments have been carefully noted. Yours sincerely,

lan Philps
Office of the Leader of the Opposition.

22. Right Honourable Ruth Kelly, Labour MP for Bolton West - Secretary of
Sate for Education:

No reply has been received yet – Is it a Parliamentary convention?

23. From the Right Honourable Oliver Letwin, Conservative MP for West
Dorest - Shadow Secretary of Sate for Environment, Food and Rural
Affairs (11 July 2005):

Dear Mr. Roberto,

Many thanks for your letter of 1 July.

I am afraid that I do not believe that the current problems in
Zimbabwe have been caused by the UK or other Western countries.
On the contrary, I believe that they have been caused by President
Mugabe's mistaken policies.

Oliver Letwin.

24. From Mr Andrew George, Liberal Democrats MP for St Ives (12 July
2005)

Letter a):

Dear Zimi Roberto,

RE: ZIMBABWE

Thank you for your letter of 1st July 2005 and I am grateful to you
for your comments and interpretations of the situation in Africa
and in Zimbabwe in particular.

It appears that the primary questions are directed at Kate Hoey MP.

I think that the Parliamentary record of the debate you refer to really speaks for itself, though I appreciate there will be many different people with very different experiences and interpretations they
would wish to add. I was certainly interested to read about yours.

However, the primary purpose and focus of the debate, as I recol-
lect, was the context of Zimbabwean asylum applicants in Britain.

I assume, from what you say, that these asylum applicants have nothing to fear from being returned to Zimbabwe. I am sorry that we will have to disagree on this point.

With my very best wishes.

cc: Kate Hoey MP.

From Mr ANDREW GEORGE MP
Letter b):

9th December 2005

Please Quote Ref: 05/23.1/ag/ew

Dear Zimi Roberto,

RE: CHINESE PRESIDENT'S VISIT TO UK

Thank you for your letter dated 8th November 2005 and for your comments regarding the state visit of China's President to Britain. I do apologise for my delay in replying.

It appears that your letter will have been circulated more widely and I suspect that this will have included my Parliamentary colleague, the Liberal Democrat Shadow Foreign Secretary - Rt. Hon Sir Menzies Campbell MP – who will have appreciated your comments on this matter.

With every good wish.

Yours sincerely,

cc: Rt. Hon Sir Menzies Campbell MP

25. From Mr Peter Bottomley Esq., Conservative MP Worthing West: Zimi Roberto

10th November 2005

PB/BC

Thank you for your letter of 8th November regarding human rights in China and Hu

Jintao's visit to London.

I share many of your concerns about democracy and human rights. As a Member of

Parliament, it would be inappropriate for me to directly participate in any protests that

take place. I did, however, sign Early Day Motion (EDM) 834 on 24th October, which called for the police to facilitate peaceful protests against human rights abuses and ensure that Hu Jintao is not prevented from seeing any protests. On the 271 October, I signed Liam Fox's EDM 883, condemning Chinese infringements on human rights in Tibet. In July, EDM 630 drew attention to the fact that rapid economic change in China has not been matched by political or social reform and called on the British government to press their Chinese counterparts to practice greater tolerance of religious organisations.

I will continue to monitor the situation in China closely, and take appropriate action wherever possible.

Thank you for writing.

Peter Bottomley MP

26. Mr John McDonnell Esq. Labour MP for Hayes & Harlington:

No reply has been received yet – is it a Parliamentary convention?

27. Mr Ian Pearson Esq., Labour MP - Minister of State (Trade), Foreign & Commonwealth Office:

No reply has been received yet – is it a Parliamentary convention?

28. Mr William Cash Esq. Conservative MP for Stone:

No reply has been received yet – is it a Parliamentary convention?

29. Mr William McCrea Esq. Democratic Unionist MP for South Antrim:

No reply has been received yet – is it a Parliamentary convention?

30. Mrs Cheryl Gillan, Conservative MP for Chesham and Amersham:

No reply has been received yet – is it a Parliamentary convention?

31. From Right Honourable Peter Hain, Labour MP for Neath and Secretary of State for Wales (05 July 2005):

Only a House of Commons' Acknowledgement card was received.

32. Right Hon. Patricia Hewitt, Labour MP for Leicester West – Secretary of State for Health:

No reply has been received yet – is it a Parliamentary convention?

33. Right Honourable Iain Duncan Smith, Conservative MP for Chingford and Woodford Green:

No reply has been received yet – is it a Parliamentary convention?

34. From Mr. Tim Yeo Esq. Con MP for South Suffolk – Shadow Secretary of State for Environment and Transport

8 August 2005

Thank you for your letter of 5 July.

I was interested in your comments about the causes of poverty in Africa.

Clearly these go beyond the problems of bad governments and corruption to which I made reference to on the Adam Boulton programme recently. Nevertheless, I do not believe that they will be solved unless corruption and bad governance is also eliminated.

I have had a long-standing interest in issues relating to the developing world. I chose to spend my gap year before going to Cambridge University in a remote part of southern Tanzania, at that time one of the poorest regions in east Africa.

I am planning to return there early next year to examine how much conditions have or have not improved in the intervening years.

35. From Andrew Tsolaki, on behalf of Rit. Hon. Baroness Amos, Leader of
the House of Lords (23 June 2005):

Dear Zimi Roberto,

"Baroness Amos has asked me to thank you for your letter of the
23rd June 2005. The issues you raise fall within the responsibilities
of the Foreign and Commonwealth Office. I have therefore passed
your letter to them for reply.

Yours sincerely

Andrew Tsolaki
Support Officer to Baroness Amos.

36. Miss Julie Kirkbride, Conservative MP for Bromsgrove:

No reply has been received yet – is it a Parliamentary convention?

37. Mr David Cameron, leader of Conservative party in opposition:

A reply from Fiona Melville, The Cameron Campaign
Ref: FM/nm/R

14th November, 2005

Dear Zimi Roberto

David Cameron has asked me to thank you for your recent letter
and to reply on his behalf. As you can imagine, he is receiving a
very large number of letters at the moment and he is very sorry that
he cannot reply to each one himself.

Your comments have been noted. I do hope you will keep in touch
with the campaign, including policy proposals, via our web-site,
www.cameroncampaign.org.

Yours sincerely

Fiona Melville
The Cameron Campaign

38. From Mr L Hudson, Ministerial Correspondence Unit, on behalf of the

Lord Falconer, Secretary of State:

Department for Constitutional Affairs Justice, rights and democracy
Ministerial Correspondence Unit

Dear Zimi Roberto,

Transferred Letter
Our Reference: 192313-1

Date: 23 November 2005

Thank you for your letter of 22 November 2005 addressed to the
Lord Falconer, Secretary of State; it was received here 23 November
2005.

The issue raised is outside the remit of this department.
Consequently, I have forwarded your letter to the Foreign and
Commonwealth Office, so that they can consider its contents.

If you wish, you can contact the Foreign and Commonwealth
Office (FCO) on:

020 7008 1500 / 020 7008 2795; or at
Allocation Section
King Charles Street,
London SW1 A 2AH

Yours sincerely

MR L HUDSON
Ministerial Correspondence Unit
cc: Transferee.

39. Dr Liam Fox, Conservative MP for Woodspring and then contender for
Conservative leadership:

No reply has been received yet – is it a Parliamentary convention?

40. Right Honourable David Davis – Conservative MP for Haltemphire and
Howden and Shadow Secretary of State for Home Office:

No reply has been received yet – is it a Parliamentary convention?

41. From Right Honourable Malcolm Rifkind – Conservative MP for Kensington and Chelsea and then contender for Conservative leadership:

    Only a House of Commons' Acknowledgement card was received.

42. Right Honourable Theresa May – Conservative MP for Maidenhead and Party Chairwoman:

    No reply has been received yet – is it a Parliamentary convention?

43. From Right Honourable Kenneth Clarke – Conservative MP for Rushcliffe and then contender for Conservative leadership:

    House of Commons' Acknowledgement card was received.

44. Right Honourable John Redwood – Conservative MP for Wokingham:

    No reply has been received yet – is it a Parliamentary convention?

45. Ms Karen Buck – Labour MP for Regent's Park and Kensington North:

    No reply has been received yet – is it a Parliamentary convention?

46. Right Honourable Ann Widdecombe – Conservative MP for Maidstone and the Weald and former Shadow Secretary of State for Home Office:

    No reply has been received yet – is it a Parliamentary convention?

47. Right Honourable George Young – Conservative MP for North West Hampshire:

    No reply has been received yet – is it a Parliamentary convention?

48. Mr Alan Duncan – Conservative MP for Rutland and Melton and Shadow Secretary of State for Trade and Industry:

    No reply has been received yet – is it a Parliamentary convention?

49. Mr David Willetts – Conservative MP for Havant and Shadow Secretary of State for Education and Skills:

No reply has been received yet – is it a Parliamentary convention?

50. From Right Honourable Charles Kennedy – former Liberal Democratic Party leader:

House of Commons' Acknowledgement card was received.

As we can grasp, throughout this chapter, Westminster concern in Zimbabwe has been related to the missing values of Western liberal democracy and human rights in Africa. These missing values need to be lectured to Africans by Westminster's evangelists. Some British MPs seem to believe that they are elected to the House of Commons because they unanimously have the 'star quality' to represent not only their own constituencies, but also to extend their representations to the nations of Africa and elsewhere. With morally unfit representatives within this British political institution, many MPs still proud in giving a false impression to other nations outside the Western world that they are endowed with high moral quality and principles, as well as they are some of the finest moral evangelists on the world stage. They are wrong because they are merely hypocrites, charlatans and liars. For instance, how can an important and one of the main Britain's opposition political parties, the Liberal Democratic Party engage in moral issues with morally unsuitable representatives? I do not refer to Mr Charles Kennedy, former Liberal Democrat leader who was forced by a handful of his party members to resign from the party on account of his drinking problem without anyone exploring his individual conduct and approach towards the aims and objective of the party. I have a deferential respect for Mr Kennedy for what he has achieved for his party in recent years. I am simply referring to the hirer of rent boys (male prostitutes), hypocrites and homosexual liars, and so forth. How can such a party impart the notion of British moral principles with Africa and the rest of the world? Mark Oaten, Liberal Democratic Home Affairs spokesman, resigned over sex scandals. Oaten, 41, married with two daughters, had been in a relationship involving a 23-year-old male from 2004 to 2005, in which £80 was the price paid by the MP for each time he enjoyed gay sex, and on one occasion, he paid £140 to enjoy three-in-bed gay sex. Another Liberal Democrat, Mr Simon Hughes, single, 54, also admitted to The Sun newspaper that he was also gay. More importantly, he explained that he was NOT the only MP at Westminster who is secretly gay. Hughes would not dare to declare that he was not the only secret gay within the British political community if he did not know of others in the same situation. He has left the impression that these other secret gays will be exposed in due course. These are merely a fraction of the sicknesses at the centre of the British Parliament.

But there are other scandals, though in some instances the indecent British Members of Parliament pretend to be the vanguard promoters and educators of moral and ethical values on the world stage. Behaviour of this nature is accommodating to MPs with a history of drug use (a concrete example is that of an evasive young David Cameron, Conservative leader – I come back to the issue of his past illegal drug use at the end of this paragraph), adultery, prostitute hiring, infidelity, perjury, lies and half-truths, corruption, swindler, greed, hypocrisy, pomposity, and many other indecent and immoral vices – these are regrettable and shameful developments that have diminished the pride and dignity of the British Parliament. (I recommend readers to read the book called *'Great Parliamentary Scandals – Four Centuries of Calumny, Smear and Innuendo'* – first published in 1995 – by Matthew Parris)

By being too evasive over the issue of his past illegal drug use and limiting his defence on the individual right to private past, instead of admitting his unfit past moral behaviour, the Tory leader, young David Cameron sets an appalling and shocking example which that encourages not only the serious scourge of illegal drugs intakes within British society, but also sets a green light for young people to do whatever they want in their youth period, and when they enter a pubic sphere, they simply seek their right to private past and move on even to becoming a British Prime Minister. Further to this, as many British MPs feel that Africa remains as an easy place in the world where they can promulgate Western moral values, it is worth to urge David Cameron that setting his feet in Africa for this purpose will be regarded as Western paradoxical and mocking attitude. Taking into consideration the Tory leader's recent reaction over the issue of his past illegal drug intakes, it is evident that on moral issues or on how African politicians can implement those values for the benefit of their societies, Cameron has got nothing to lecture Africans and in particular young African people.

If Mark Oaten had become leader of the Liberal Democratic Party, what would he impart or teach Africans on moral and ethical issues?

Most people will not tolerate bad governance and corruption because these are the evils of society, however, they are temporary issues that can be addressed and defeated. But African people would be offended and shocked to learn of an African government run by hirers of homosexual prostitutes. I am not against any sexual orientation, but it is deeply regrettable to have within Westminster MPs who hide their sexual orientation for political reason, while simultaneously they want to be our evangelists on moral and ethical values. Whereas, taking into consideration the above scandals and others, the moral credibility of many British MPs at Westminster has to be called into question.

Looking at the issues of Western liberal democracy and freedom of expression that Westminster's evangelists are devoted to spreading across the world, for instance, what can African politicians learn from British politics when free expression is required of Africans, but the same free expression value is oppressed or controlled in a particular political manner within Labour party?

There have been several complaints on how freedom and liberty are suppressed in the British political system. The remarkable ones have included the serious protests/complaints made over the stewards' heavy-handed method Walter Wolfgang, the 82-year-old Labour member was grabbed out as mad dog from Labour conference hall in Brighton, after shouting "nonsense", and accusing the former Foreign Secretary Mr Jack Straw of lying over the Iraq war. Another Labour member, who complained about the brutal treatment to the tired old man, was also lifted from his feet and ejected out of the conference hall. This is similar to the brutal method used by the US police, which has been criticised by the United Nations for many years.

Now, the paradox is that if similar incidents happen in any ZANU-PF conference in Zimbabwe, they would automatically be blamed on the so-called "Mugabe's coterie of gangsters", and we would see compassionate British politicians and promoters of the international justice, such as Kate Hoey, Richard Benyon, Michael Ancram, Jack Straw and many others rushing to the TV screens, Internet and newspapers, to hijack the incident and blow it out of proportion to the British public. They would fuel the incident, thus creating a pretext to intervene in the internal affairs of Zimbabwe and viciously exhorting a British "resolute action" against Mugabe's Government; they would use alarmist language aimed at inflaming division in Zimbabwe and calling for US/European Union isolation of ZANU-PF. Indeed, this is all the more true of the power of Western imperialist and neo-colonialist propaganda machine that has since been dictating Africa.

Finally, to understand President Roberto Mugabe's resentment to British neo-colonialist policy towards Zimbabwe (resentment that sometimes is interpreted by Westminster to be of racist nature), let me bring to British MPs an interesting and emotional reminiscent historical fact: according to Geoff Hill, in his book called 'The Battle for Zimbabwe – The Final Countdown – 2003,' during Zimbabwean colonial era, Bona Mugabe, President Mugabe's mother was helping out at the Jesuit mission in Katuma (birth place of Mugabe) founded ten years earlier by a French priest, Jean-Baptiste Loubiére. President Robert Mugabe and his brothers began their education at that very same mission, which had been then taken over after Loubiére died in 1930 by an Irish priest, Father O'Hea, who had nothing but contempt for the colonial government in Salisbury (Harare); he was committed to the need of his flock to blend Christianity with traditional beliefs. Geoff asserts that O'Hea came from a wealthy family, and used his own money to expand primary education at the mission and to build a school where he could train the most promising students to become future teachers. But the Irish priest thought that it was also indispensable need to have a local hospital in Katuma. To see his dream through, O'Hea turned to the government in Salisbury (actual Harare) for help, inviting the then Prime Minister, Godfrey Huggins, to visit Katuma and see for himself the work being done there. The then colonial Governor, Cecil Rodwell, who according to Geoff was nothing more than a figurehead, accompanied the Prime Minister in his visit to Katuma, and in the presence of the young Robert Mugabe, then aged only nine, he asked the priest this: *"Why he was so passionate about the idea of healing the sick"* – after that, he added: *"there are so many natives in the country already"*. Again, according to Geoff, *"Mugabe neither forgot nor forgave the comment."*

CHAPTER THREE

CHAPTER TEN

THREE

LACK OF HONOURABLE INTEREST IN AFRICA WITHIN THE HOUSE OF COMMONS – A RESEARCH WORK

I undertook this research project to broaden the horizons of many readers' understanding of British Members of Parliament (MPs), who have been deceptively trying to please blind Africans when debating about Africa's affairs in the House of Commons. When a politician ascends to the rank of President or Prime Minister, it has become an accepted fact in the US and UK politics that their desire is not only to lead their own people, but sometimes to overstep their responsibilities and govern the whole world, particularly the backwater continent, Africa. After centuries of dehumanising Africa's colonisation by Europeans, some politicians have today been self-promoted to champions of the African people's cause, lecturing at great lengths on Western liberal democratic and human rights values to African who have been the victims of human rights abuse during Africa's colonization.

Many Africans have found it interesting to note that Mr Blair and many British politicians at Westminster, even those who had never set foot in Africa's soil before, have been subscribing themselves as promoters of the African cause and acting as vanguards for the struggle to defeat one of Africa's greatest evils, "poverty". This partially ignores the fact that the man-made poverty of Africa is a product of European greed.

More importantly, this research is about British MPs' lack of moral and faithful interest in Africa. In publishing this research in this book, I propose to draw the readers' attention to the British Parliamentarians' obscure attitude to Africa's problems, and, moreover, make readers aware of how many British MPs have been apathetic to Africa and its people. It is important too to mention about those MPs, who, after the Cold War had ended in the favour of the West in 1989/90, had hypocritically and viciously turned the blame on African leaders for lack of liberal democracy, human rights abuses, corruption, incompetence, and so forth. Many of those MPs have never been interested in African people and their crucial continental affairs in any way, except so as to safeguard British economic interests in any part of the African continent and with no regard to African resolution. Furthermore, as emphasised in the previous chapter, the young African nation of Zimbabwe has been the most concrete example of this Western imperialistic approach towards Africa. The established directory: 'Dod's Parliamentary Companion 2003' – by Vacher Dod Publishing Ltd, explores the biography of each British MP. My research on this publication focuses on those countries of the world that interest British MPs, with particular regard to their interests in African countries. Through this publication it is uncovered the following information:

- Out of 659 British MPs, only 117 of them were interested in one or more countries in Africa. It means that some of them were only interested in commonwealth and British overseas territories, some in French-speaking Africa, some in a particular African region, and others were interested in Africa as a whole, including also those who were interested in all developing countries or all small nations of the world. Out of the 117 MPs (interested in African countries): 71 were from the Labour party, 30 from the Conservative party, 13 from the Liberal Democrats and three from other parties.

- Out of 659 British MPs, 268 had no preference or had chosen not to do so, probably for political and diplomatic reasons to publicly unveil their countries of interest. Out of this number with no preference: 158 were from the Labour Party, 70 from the Conservative Party, 25 from the Liberal Democrats and 15 from other parties.

- Interestingly, out of 659 British MPs, although 144 were interested in countries other than Africa, all of them were also interested in the USA. And, more interestingly, out of these 144 MPs, seven British MPs (all male) were only interested in the USA rather than in any other country in Europe or in the world; of this number, 6 were from the Conservative party alone and one from the Liberal Democrats. These were:

1. Right Honourable Michael Howard, MP for Folkestone and Hythe, former Secretary of Sate for the Home Office, former shadow Secretary of State for Foreign Affairs and former Conservative party leader, embarrassingly defeated at the last British general election.

2. Right Honourable John Redwood, Conservative MP for Wokingham,

who had contested for and was defeated in the Conservative leadership in 1995 and 1997 during the era of John Major as British Prime Minister. Redwood has also been among the British elites who disingenuously blames African leaders for Africa's corruption and lack of democracy – I want to come back to him in the next chapter.

3. Right Honourable Michael Spicer, Conservative MP for West Worcestershire.

4. Right Honourable Simon Burns, Conservative MP for Chelmsford West.

5. Right Honourable Greg Knight, Conservative MP for Yorkshire Fast.

6. Right Honourable John Mark Taylor, Conservative MP for Solihull.

7. Right Honourable Adrian Sanders, Liberal Democratic MP for Torbay.

Let me bring here the Right Honourable Michael Jack, Conservative MP for Fylde. His countries of interest are China, USA and Italy. His political interests are Economic Issues, Energy, Nuclear Industry, Horticulture, Sheltered Housing, Aerospace, Transport, Agriculture. In one of the recent Prime Minister question time at the House of Commons, he questioned Blair on what his Commission was doing when people in Zimbabwe were still suffering. He claimed that there was a person who was arrested just for selling tomatoes in a street corner. On the one hand, Zimbabwe does not make-up the list of his countries of interest in this world. On the other hand, if the arrest of a poor tomatoes' trader by a disobedient police in Zimbabwe becomes an issue to add up to motives for 'no-aid' to Zimbabwe, it would mean that all African countries could be liable to 'no-aid' from Blair's comprehensive aid package to Africa. It is not pleasant and I do not condone that a poor individual trading tomatoes be arrested, unless it is done according to Zimbabwean trading law. Mr Jack appears to make us believe that an arrest of a tomatoes' trader in Zimbabwe is more serious than the brutal manner Mr Walter Wolfgang, an 82-year-old loyal Labour supporter was driven out from the Labour conference hall in Brighton. He also seems to give the impression that an arrest of a tomatoes' trader in Zimbabwe is more serious than a British police shooting to kill an innocent Brazilian Jean Charles de Menezes – the poor man was shot 8 times in the head as a "mad dog" because of being suspected of a terrorist on 22nd of July 2005. Undisciplined or disobedient police is typical not only in all African police ranks but everywhere in the world. I simply invite the Right Honourable Michael Jack to tour other African countries than Zimbabwe and come back to tell the British House of Commons that he had not found any undisciplined or disobedient police. We have many of them in Britain.

In addition, this research has uncovered that the man who told his party to "unite or die" after being angered by his party colleagues over his poor political performance in the House Commons – the man who has self-proclaimed as "quite man", an ever unsuccessful former Conservative party leader who very briefly led the party, the then Right Honourable Ian Duncan Smith, Conservative MP for Chingford and Woodford Green, in the past served as a Commander of Commonwealth Monitoring Force in Zimbabwe between 1979 and 1981. Although the historical ties that exist between Zimbabwe and Britain, he has not been interested in Zimbabwe or any other African country. His four countries of interest are USA, Italy, India and Sri Lanka. His continental countries do not interest him, but the USA does. And surprisingly, when I checked in the updated 'Dod's Parliamentary Companion 2005', I found that Duncan Smith had removed all his countries of interest in the world. I suspect that in the course of 2004, Duncan Smith might have been informed by other MPs of my research project on their countries of interest. On 01 July 2005, I thought it proper to write and ask him why he had removed the four countries that had interested him from his biography; and to also ask him if there was a particular reason for doing so. The former Tory leader has not yet replied to my request. Additionally, and more interestingly, there is a remarkable change in the 2006 edition of 'Dod's Parliamentary Companion'. In the biography part of the book, it no longer asks for countries of interest as it did in the previous editions; instead, political interest question now covers countries of interest. For instance, let us explore Duncan Smith's biography and the changes that have occurred in the Dod's Parliamentary Companion between the 2003 and 2006, focusing merely in his countries of interest in the world:

a) 2003 biography:

DUNCAN SMITH, IAIN Chingford and Woodford Green Con majority 5487

(George) Ian Duncan Smith. Born 9 April 1954; Son of late Group Captain W. G. G. Duncan Smith, DSO, DFC, and Pamela, née Summers; Educated HMS Conway (Cadet School); University of Perugia, Italy; RMA Sandhurst; Dunchurch College of Management; Married Hon. Elizabeth Wynne Fremantle 1982

(2 sons 2 daughters). Commissioned, Scots Guards 1975; ADC
to Major-General Sir John Acland, KCB, CBE, Commander of
Commonwealth Monitoring Force in Zimbabwe 1979-81; GEC
Marconi 1981; Director: Bellwinch Property1988-89, Publishing
Director Jane's Information Group 1989-92. **House of Commons:**
Contested Bradford West 1987 general election. Member for
Chingford 1992-97, and for Chingford and Woodford Green since
May 1, 1997; Member, Shadow Cabinet 1997-; Shadow secretary
of State for: Social Security 1997-99, Defence 1999-2001; Leader
of the Opposition 2001-: Leader, Conservative party 2001-; *Select
Committees*: Member: Administration 1993-97, Health 1993-95,
Standards and Privileges 1995-97. *Special Interests*: Finance, Small
Businesses, Transport, Defence, Environment. *Countries of Interest:*
India, Italy, Sri Lanka, USA. Vice-Chair, Fulham Conservative
Association 1991; Chair Conservative Policy Board 2001-.
Publications: Co-author *Who Benefits? Reinventing Social Security;
Game, Set and Match?* (Maastricht); *Facing the Future* (Defence and
Foreign and Commonwealth Affairs); *1994 and Beyond; A Response
to Chancellor Kohl; A Race Against time, Europe's growing vulnerabil-
ity to missile attack 2002*; PC 2001; Freeman, City of London 1993;
Recreations: Cricket, Rugby, tennis, sport in general, painting, the-
atre, family. Rit Hon Iain Duncan Smith, MP, House of Commons,
London, SW1A 0AA. *Constituency:* 20A Station Road, Chingford,
London, E4 7BE *Tel*: 020 8524 4344.

Iain Duncan Smith's 2004 biography remained the same as above. But
his biography in 2005 was altered. His all 4 countries of interest were removed from his biography. See below:

b) 2005 biography:

DUNCAN SMITH, IAIN Chingford and Woodford Green Con
majority 5487

(George) Ian Duncan Smith. Born 9 April 1954; Son of late
Group Captain W. G. G. Duncan Smith, DSO, DFC, and
Pamela, née Summers; Educated HMS Conway (Cadet School);
University of Perugia, Italy; RMA Sandhurst; Dunchurch College
of Management; Married Hon. Elizabeth Wynne Fremantle 1982
(2 sons 2 daughters). Commissioned, Scots Guards 1975; ADC
to Major-General Sir John Acland, KCB, CBE, Commander of

Commonwealth Monitoring Force in Zimbabwe 1979-81; GEC
Marconi 1981; Director: Bellwinch Property1988-89, Publishing
Director Jane's Information Group 1989-92. **House of Commons:**
Contested Bradford West 1987 general election. Member for
Chingford 1992-97, and for Chingford and Woodford Green since
May 1, 1997; Member, Shadow Cabinet 1997-; Shadow secretary
of State for: Social Security 1997-99, Defence 1999-2001; Leader
of the Opposition 2001-: Leader, Conservative party 2001-; *Select
Committees*: Member: Administration 1993-97, Health 1993-95,
Standards and Privileges 1995-97. *Political Interests*: Finance, Small
Businesses, Transport, Defence, Environment. Vice-Chair, Fulham
Conservative Association 1991; Chair Conservative Policy Board
2001-. *Publications*: Co-author *Who Benefits? Reinventing Social
Security; Game, Set and Match?* (Maastricht); *Facing the Future*
(Defence and Foreign and Commonwealth Affairs); *1994 and
Beyond; A Response to Chancellor Kohl; A Race Against time, Europe's
growing vulnerability to missile attack 2002*; PC 2001; Freeman,
City of London 1993; *Recreations*: Cricket, Rugby, tennis, sport
in general, painting, theatre, family. Rit Hon Iain Duncan Smith,
MP, House of Commons, London, SW1A 0AA. *Constituency:* 20A
Station Road, Chingford, London, E4 7BE *Tel*: 020 8524 4344.
Website: www.epolitix.com/Iain-Duncan Smith.

Iain Duncan Smith's 2006 biography remains the same as above.

Yet, and more interestingly, when I wrote to the Rt. Hon. Frank Dobson,
Lab MP for Holborn on 01 July 2005, asking him why he has chosen South
Africa as his only country of interest in Africa, in his replying letter to me
dated 06 July 2005, the last paragraph says this:

"However, in acknowledging receipt of your letter, I would ask you
to let me know from where you gained the impression that I have
no interest in Africa. This, quite simply, is not true".

Now, let us look at Frank Dobson 2005 biography and explore the altera-
tion noted in his 2006 biography, after his above reaction to my letter over his
countries of interest. See bellow:

a) 2005 biography:

DOBSON, FRANK Holborn and St Pancras Lab majority 11,175

Frank Dobson, Born 15 March 1940; Son of late James William
Dobson, railwayman, and late Irene Dobson; Educated Archbishop
Holgate's Grammar School, York; London School of Economics
(BSc(Econ) 1962); Married Janet Mary Alker 1967 (1 daughter
2 sons). Worked at HQ of: CEGB 1962-70, Electricity Council
1970-75; Assistant Secretary, Office of Local Ombudsman 1975-
79; RMT. Camden Borough Council: Councillor 1971 76, Leader
of the Council 1973-75. **House of Commons:** Member for
Holborn and St Pancras since May 1979; Opposition Spokesperson
for Education 1981-83; Principal Opposition Spokesperson for:
Energy 1989-92, Employment 1992-93, Transport and London
1993-94, Environment and London 1994-97; Shadow Health
Minister 1983-87; Shadow Leader, House of Commons and
Campaigns Co-ordinator 1987-89; Shadow Energy Secretary 1989-
92; Shadow Employment secretary 1992-93; Shadow Transport
Secretary 1993-94; Shadow Minister for London 1993-97; Shadow
Environment Secretary1994-97; Secretary of State for Health
1997-99; *Political Interests*: Problems of central London, Transport,
Energy, Redistribution of wealth, Government Reform. *Countries
of Interest:* South Africa, Bangladesh. Chair, Network South Africa
2004; PC 1997; Clubs: Covent Garden Community centre;
Recreations: Walking, theatre, watching cricket and football.

Rt Hon Frank Dobson, MP, House of Commons, London SW1A
0AA *Tel:* 020 7219 6956. *Constituency:* 8 Camden Road, London
NW1 9DP *Te;* 020 7267 1676 *Fax:* 020 7482 3950 *E-mail:* col-
linsb@parliament.uk

b) 2006 biography:
DOBSON, FRANK Holborn and St Pancras (Majority 4,787)

Frank Dobson. Born 15 March 1940; Son of late James William
Dobson, railwayman, and late Irene Dobson; Educated Archbishop
Holgate's Grammar School, York; London School of Economics
(BSc(Econ) 1962); Married Dr Janet Mary Alker 1967 (1 daughter
2 sons). Worked at HQ of: CEGB 1962-70, Electricity Council
1970-75; Assistant Secretary, Office of Local Ombudsman 1975-
79; RMT; Camden Borough Council: Councillor 1971-76, Leader
of the Council 1973-75

House of Commons: Member for Holborn and St Pancras since

3 May 1979 general election; Opposition Spokesperson for
Education 1981-83; Principal Opposition Spokesperson for:
Energy 1989-92, Employment 1992-93, Transport and London
1993-94, Environment and London 1994-97; Shadow Health
Minister 1983-87; Shadow Leader, House of Commons and
Campaigns Co-ordinator 1987-89; Shadow: Energy Secretary
1989-92, Employment Secretary 1992-93, Transport Secretary
1993-94, Minister for London 1993-97, Environment Secretary
1994-97; Secretary of State for Health 1997-99; *Select Committees*:
Member: Administration 2005-. *Political Interests*: Problems of
Central London, Transport, Energy, Redistribution of Wealth,
Government Reform, South Africa, Bangladesh

Chair, Network South Africa 2004; PC 1997; *Clubs*: Covent
Garden Community Centre; *Recreations*: Walking, theatre, watching cricket and football

Rt Hon Frank Dobson, MP, House of Commons, London SW1A
0AA
Tel: 020 7219 5040 *Fax*: 020 7219 6956 *E-mail*: <u>collinsb@parlia-</u>
<u>ment.uk</u>
Constituency: 8 Camden Road, London NW1 9DP *Tel*: 020 7267
1676
Fax: 020 7482 3950

Having explored the above British MPs biographies, I propose to the
readers to make their own assessment as to whether the alterations made in
Duncan Smith and Frank Dobson biographies in the course of 2005 and
2006 have been unintended or accidental. However, according to my own
perspective, taking also into consideration my genuine criticism of Michael
Howard and other British MPs in this chapter, there is a strong suspicion
which indicates that some of the British MPs I wrote to have exerted pressure on Dod's Parliamentary Companion publisher to remove the request for
countries of interest on British MPs' biographies.

Furthermore, this research also found that one British official who had
occupied a high-ranking position at the Home Office had publicly disclosed
her countries of interest or preference. This is the Right Honourable Barbara
Roche, Labour MP for Hornsey and Wood Green, formerly, Minister of State
for the Home Office, who was interested in only two countries, Cyprus and
Israel. However, this book does not plan to discuss at length what might be
the implications or sentiments in the Arab world for a Home Office Minister

at top-ranking British politics to publicly declare that Israel is his or her single country of interest in the Middle East.

In contrast, however, this research project uncovered, that most high-ranking Labour Cabinet members, including former members, had no countries of interest/preference or had chosen not to disclose them publicly, presumably for political and diplomatic reasons, thereby, avoiding the world's criticism and resentment. These Labour Cabinet officials include the members: Tony Blair, John Prescott, Gordon Brown, David Blunkett, Jack Straw, Margaret Beckett, Alistair Darling, John Reid and former cabinet members, Clare Short, Stephen Byers, Estelle Morris and the late Robin Cook. Where the high-ranking members of the Conservative party are concerned, and, for those reasons given above, the list includes: Michael Ancram, David Davis, Theresa May, William Hague, former Conservative party leader and current Conservative Shadow Secretary of State for foreign Affairs, Michael Portillo, former shadow Chancellor of the Exchequer, and Ann Widdecombe, former shadow Secretary of State for the Home Office. Charles Kennedy, the former leader of the Liberal Democrats has adopted the same position in terms of countries of interest. Gerry Adams, Sinn Fein leader and David Trimble, former Ulster Union party leader adopted the same attitude.

As international politics stands today, it is a matter of both deep regret and precarious in modern Britain to have a British Prime Minister and high-ranking British politicians who occupy top government positions expressing publicly that the USA is their only country of preference rather than any country within their own continent, Europe. The "no to European Constitution" advocated by Michael Howard and many other British politicians came at no surprise to many people and politicians across Europe. It reminds us of General Charles De Gaulle's vetoes to Britain's applications to the European Economic Community (EEC), made respectively by Harold Macmillan (Conservative) in 1963 and Harold Wilson (Labour) in 1967. De Gaulle's vetoes were reflected on the fear that British membership would eventually bring the Anglo-American influence and interests into the EEC. De Gaulle also foresaw a feasible massive Atlantic Community block under American domination; moreover, according to the SIX state members of EEC (Germany, France, Italy, Belgium, Luxemburg and the Netherlands), British membership would only bring a dramatic change to the structure of their then newly established organisation, which was already operating successfully. De Gaulle's suspicion was quite understandable owing to the fact that at the inception of EC (European Community), which later changed to European Economic Community), Britain was not interested to integrate with other European countries, and therefore, it stayed remotely detached from the European integration project, as Michael Howard's position to the European Constitution has been manifested recently. But earlier in the sixties, Britain realised that British trade in Europe was beneficial as the economies of the SIX were performing well, and it decided to join. Unfortunately, both applications for European Community (EC) membership were vetoed by General De Gaulle.

However, this book is not a review of the history and development of the European Union; it is about what matters for Africans. The research outlined here may shed light to many people on Western politicians' façades when they pretend to champion Africa's cause. We can be faithfully and highly motivated to other people's cause only if we really are interested in them and their problems. No the other way round. Therefore, in the next chapter, I will again refute the comments made by Michael Howard on world free trade and his pledge for Africa; I will challenge the deceitful comments made by Michael Ancram on food shortage in Zimbabwe; I will tackle the disingenuous comments made by John Redwood and Tim Yeo's on African corruption at a June BBC Question Time TV and Adam Boulton's Sky News programmes. I also want to challenge Mr David Wnnick's, Labour MP, over his flattery comments to the British Prime Minister in the House of Commons, 10 December 2003.

Finally, it is open to readers to add any further suggestions and a conclusion to this research enterprise.

CHAPTER FOUR

CHAPTER XIX

FOUR

MY CRITICISM OF DISINGENUOUS BRITISH PARLIAMENTARIANS/ POLITICIANS

> To our regret, Africa's suffering has become an opportunity to unfaithfully be explored by dishonest British politicians in order to win some additional votes from ethnic minority, and then make their road to Number 10 Downing Street. (Statement by Africans)

1. MY CRITICISM OF RIGHT HONOURABLE MICHAEL HOWARD—MP FOR FOLKESTONE AND HYTHE AND FORMER CONSERVATIVE PARTY LEADER.

Mr Howard cannot be allowed to mislead ordinary African people with his compassionate words. The fact is that his only country of interest is the USA rather than any other country in Europe or in the rest of the world. When it is expected that the former Conservative leader, many other politicians and media should know that based on the awareness of Africa's reality in the West, little has been done in good faith to tackle the crucial causes leading to Africa's poverty – instead, what has been seen on Western TV screens and read in many newspapers across the countries of the West seems to suggest, since European colonists left Africa, poverty in the continent can be cured with endless compassionate words and a flood of broken Western promises. I therefore was neither impressed nor surprised when, in early March 2004, the Right Honourable Michael Howard misleadingly criticised the USA for devastating the world trade. This was a gimmick that has become one of the patterns for British politicians to please the world poorest countries and British voters, especially voters from minority communities, so they can be given green light to make their road to Number 10 Downing Street. To many less fair-minded people, it may appear that Howard has been faithful to the poorer nations of the world and vehemently blames Washington for imposing trade barriers which hamper development and prosperity in the Third

World. However, more interestingly, it possibly went unnoticed to many less-vigilant people that Howard was employing his political tricks only 4 days after Tony Blair announced his suspicious and gimmick pledge to champion the African people' s cause during the February 2004 Prime Ministerial press conference.

From what we know about the aftermath of an illegal and unpopular war in Iraq, which both Blair and Howard overwhelmingly supported, it was unequivocal that while Blair was turning to Africa's poverty as an opportunity to deflect the British people's attention from his historical and political blunder in Iraq, it is obvious to understand that Michael Howard's political balance was to advocate Africa's trade justice. This was a great opportunity to restore his tarnished political image too, and thereby, renew his prospect of becoming a British Premier. Eventually, we all saw how the Tory Leader failed in his last political project to become a British Prime Minister. Michael Howard at Number 10 Downing Street, never, only until we have a hot January in Britain.

But it is also peculiar that the Tory leader could seize that opportunity to talk about the US world trade policy and lecture his party members and the entire world about world free trade, as his own party was upholding protectionist policies. The British economic protectionism approach has been there for a long time, and it is widely said that most Conservative members subscribed to the British national economic protectionism and were the most eager to endorse those ideas. When Britain faced its world 'GIANT' economic rivals, for example, in the course of 1900, Conservatives upheld imperialist and economic protectionist approach as powerful tactic to maintain Britain as a leading economy in the world.

Further to this, in addressing a Tory summit in March 2004 to promote business interests, Howard stated in his own words: *"It is a terrible mistake indictment of our progress in this area that the poorest countries' share of world trade has dropped by almost a half in the last 20 years".*

Then he benevolently asked: *"But is it any wonder when those countries which advocate free trade don't always live up to their rhetoric?"*

He went on reminding his audience that: *"Subsidies to farmers in rich countries total $300bn [£160bn] a year, more than the combined income of the whole of sub-Saharan Africa"*... *"Cotton is crucial to certain west African countries".* He mentioned that for countries such as Benin, Burkina Faso, Chad, Mali and Togo, cotton is almost the commodity they can export. *"The richer countries should act in accordance with what they know to be true: Free trade spreads prosperity. Protectionism does not".*

In my research on British MPs' biographies (see previous chapter), found that the blame that Mr Howard puts on the USA' trade policy cannot be taken seriously. This is because, Howard is among those named British Parliamentarians who have chosen the USA as their only country of interest in the world and he stands out one of the most passionate admirers of that country within the British political community at Westminster. Whatever gimmicks Howard had chosen to help him win the last British general election by trying to deflect fair-minded people's attention to the real problems that affect the African continent and their causes have failed. His esoteric pledge, *"Free trade spreads prosperity. Protectionism does not"*, was not included as one of the top priorities' agenda in his Party's last election manifesto. Instead, what the public had to listen to during the Conservative Party's election campaign was tough immigration propaganda. Howard seems to take it for granted that the perseverance of unfair trade by the West has been a West's most evil that contributes to the impairment of a mutual cooperation and cohesive world community through globalisation. The inequities in the global trading system cause enormous damage to developing nations around the world, and, as he would well know, the current world economic order commanded by the West has been opposed in all developing countries.

In the international economic field, contemporary debates also centre on neo-imperialism and neo-colonialism felt in Africa. For this reason, African people have persisted with their complaint that their economic development has been for the most part determined by the developed countries through unfair trading systems, power and control over capital, and the power of multinational corporations, which have been devastating continental economies. Britain has been accused of reducing its conditional foreign aid to some of the well-selected and poorest countries of the Third World because allegedly these countries have become unfriendly or hostile to the UK and US – for example, in Africa, Zimbabwe has been a concrete case because of its land reform policy initiated in the 1990's; the West forces certain governments in the developing world to privatise their public services, such as electricity, water, education, etc, so that it can assist its Western multinational/wealthy corporations to purchase these expensive African national and public assets. As many politicians in the West believe to be the ones who know best of everything, the lecturer, Mr. Howard, would therefore know better than anyone else in the Third World that in a free-market economy, firms produce only those goods and services which are of their self-interest and profitable, with little regard to negative considerations or social costs. That is exactly why government intervention in the economy has become justified, whereas, the British economy has become more and more a mixed economy, with the government intervention seeking to keep some public sectors of the British economy under its own direct control – British health and education services are clear examples of this.

Again, with reference to Africa, and having a quick look at Africa's history, the Tory leader has deliberately avoided to mention the flood of problems that have since been devastating the continent in many ways: European colonialism and its mass exploitation of Africa's natural resources which were transported to the civilised nations of the West to sustain the long stability of their economies and social welfare systems; the massive Western trade of arms and landmines to Africa; blood trade that has left many hundreds of thousands dead and amputated; the Cold War that brought prolonged-armed conflicts to Africa, resulting in an exacerbation and a lack of trust between peoples of Africa at national, regional, and international levels; and a massive destruction of African infrastructures and loss of lives, mainly young people of labour force, thus, postponing African economic development. In his book: '*Big Men – Little People – Encounters in Africa – 1999*', Alec Russell, when elaborating on the Cold War, he provided Angola as an example of a forgotten African nation:

> Many bloodiest battles were fought thousands of miles from the superpowers in African countries which most Soviet and American citizens would not, if asked, have been able to place on a map. No one knows how many people died in Angola as sacrificial victims on the altar of superpowers politics – nor how many were mutilated by landmines which both sides sprinkled over the interior. But the answer to the first question lies somewhere in the hundreds of thousands, and the answer to the second is yet to be calculated - Angola is thought to have more landmines than its 11 million people".

In addition, among other evils that have been devastating Africa, and being compassionate to Africans, Howard did not add natural disasters, diseases, particularly the exterminating Human Immunodeficiency Virus and Acquired Immune Deficiency Syndrome (HIV/AIDS), which Nelson Mandela regards now as a real "Weapon of Mass Destruction." It is therefore important to remind the Tory leader that the black continent has been slowly dying in the eyes of richer and civilised nations, and free trade alone will not address the flood of problems facing most Africans, in particular, diseases, which have been affecting the African labour population. Indeed, in a book called '*Economic Today – the updated eighth edition*', by Roger LeRoy Miller, chapter 35 'Development Economics' reminds us:

> Throughout the world's history, disease has devastated populations

and economies. In the fourteenth century an acute infectious disease caused by the bacillus Pasteurella pestis swept through Europe
during a four-year period (1347-1351), reducing the population of
the Continent by about 35 percent. That plague set back severely
the prospects for economic development. In modern times we are
not used to thinking of plagues or other diseases as being so viru-
lent that they affect the development of nations…" Miller went on
saying that "Most Americans [presumably Michael Howard] cannot
even begin to understand the reality of poverty in the world today.
At least one-half, if not two-thirds, of the world's population lives at
subsistence level, with just enough to eat for survival - It is hard to
image, but at one time the United States [as the United Kingdom]
was a developing country. Now we are considered as developed
country. All countries that we classify as developed started out like
much of today's [so-called] Third World.

Health issues do not include only the exterminating HIV/AIDS, which
have such a high priority that they have already left millions of children orphans in Africa, but many other diseases, have also been devastating the continent for a long time. Mr Jack Chow of the World Health Organisation told
the American CNN TV channel that malaria is a number one killer in Africa.
According to his record, malaria kills one million people in the world every
single year, and of this death toll, 75% are African children under 5 years.

Also, as a European citizen and loyal friend of America, the former Tory
leader should be reminded that wars inflicted on Africa by the West have
largely benefited the West in many ways. Howard should know that in the
half a century after the Second World War and during the Cold War period,
the West has witnessed both growth and prosperity, while African continent
has succumbed to a remarkable economic decline in the last three decades.

Although it is paradoxically believed in the West that economic globalisation brings together the world community; removes trade barriers; integrates
the world economies; improves potential economic development and growth;
and may lead to world nations becoming self-sufficient and better off; however, to attain these Western economic attributes, the West should review its
dogmatic and imperialist policy towards the Third World community that it
intends to rescue, as the Americans rescued Europe in the aftermath of WWII.
The International economic institutions that organise world economic development with existing Third World economic needs and emergencies should
be in possession of world economic perfect information, particularly perfect
information from economically devastated African economies, as many eco-

nomic experts at the international financial institutions have lectured.

It is also sensible to remind Mr Howard, as it has been emphasised in my letter addressed to many British charities operating in Africa, of the following information: if lives of black African people, especially those of African children, are valued in the same way that people's lives are valued in the West, by now, British politicians and champions of the African people's cause would act without looking first at their implacable African enemies, such as Robert Mugabe or single out a group of African countries to benefit from Blair's aid to Africa.

On the contention between Westminster and Harare, Michael Howard is among many British MPs, to whom I put the same following questions:

Is President Thabo Mbeki's statement a fabrication or is he a liar too?

These are straightforward questions needing straightforward answers from British politicians, especially an easy and frank answer from Michael Howard that could shed light on the controversial relations between his country and Zimbabwe. It is interesting to remember that in the run-up to the last British general election, without any hesitation whatsoever, Howard declared his own fellow citizen, the British Prime Minister Mr Tony Blair as a "**liar**". During the electoral campaign, the Tory leader relentlessly spent consecutive 5 days branding the Prime Minister of Britain a "**liar.**" He also told the public that he had the right to highlight the Prime Minister's "**lies**" over war with Iraq in a controversial poster campaign, a political tactic that was mounting concerns amongst high ranking Tory politicians. When it was expected that President Thabo Mbeki be included in the list of world liars by Howard, instead, the former leader of Conservative party chooses not to refute or consider President Thabo Mbeki's statement as being false, and therefore, not highlighting him as an African liar.

2.   MY CRITICISM OF MR DAVID WINNICK – LABOUR MP FOR WALSALL NORTH.

As I have emphasized earlier, there are various forms of British political misrepresentations that can obscure the nature of the current social, political and economic crises in Africa. Referring to Zimbabwe in particular, this time, I would like to respond to Mr David Winnick, a Labour MP, who at a debate in the House of Commons on December 9, 2003, following the Abuja Commonwealth Heads of Government Meeting (CHOGM), asked this quoted appeasing, flattery or even impertinent question to the British Prime Minister:

Is it not the case that when Labour members campaigned continuously against the illegal regime of Smith, we were not told by Mugabe and his friends that we were anti-black. The accusation in those days of the settlers and their friends, some of whom were in the House Commons, was that we were anti-white. If a Commonwealth country that has abolished the rule of law and replaced it with outright violence were allowed to remain in the Commonwealth without any suspension, what would be the point of the Commonwealth?

Interestingly, according to Winnick's biography, the USA, Russia and China are his only countries of interest in the world. Although Winnick has no interest in African countries, however, I wrote to him on 01 July 2005, asking if he could briefly outline for me his perception of Africa as a whole and his understanding of African leaders rejecting the recent US/UK call for African Union 'AU' to intervene in the internal affairs of a sovereign African Nation of Zimbabwe. The AU has rejected the US/UK call for African Union to intervene over Government of Zimbabwe's domestic policy of '**Operation Murambatsvina' (Restore Order)** aimed at dealing with crime, squalor, and lawlessness, and rebuild and reorganize urban settlements and small and medium enterprises (SMEs) in a way that would bring dignity, order and prosperity to the stakeholders and the nation at large. Winnick has not yet replied or acknowledged my letter.

Turning to the point, at the outset, it is important to understand that the hijacking of Zimbabwe's independence by Ian Smith's UDI (Unilateral Declaration of Independence) in 1965 was not sorted out by Western economic sanctions or constitutional arrangement, and Zimbabwe's independence in 1980 was not achieved by British appeasement to black Zimbabweans, but it was achieved by the irreversible African colonial liberation struggle. Many are aware of one time in the past when African politicians were concerned for the fact that, while resolute action against the Rhodesian white minority was heard in London during the sixties and seventies, many British officials remained generous towards Ian Smith's white minority regime. For many British politicians, Ian was regarded as the Governor-General of the British colony of Rhodesia, and they were only concerned with the question of forcing Ian to reform his oppressive regime rather than abolishing it completely. In this context, having into consideration this British double standards and Tony Blair's position vis-à-vis Robert Mugabe, only leads many Africans to be suspicious of the current British resolute and draconian action against the Zimbabwe African National Union-Patriotic Front (ZANU-PF) and its leader, and an eventual "regime change" in Zimbabwe, as Blair envisages.

Getting back to history, it is pertinent for Mr Winnick to recall that when the Second World War came to an end in 1945, as has been well documented in history books, TV documentaries, newspapers, etc; on the one hand, the United Kingdom and other European colonial powers, deeply devastated and exhausted by that war, could no longer maintain its colonial occupation around the world. On the other hand, after accepting the American Marshall Plan, a financial assistance to help European countries recover their damaged economies after the war, colonial powers found that they were now vulnerable and exposed to American pressure to accelerate the decolonisation of all European colonies. Hence, seizing that opportunistic historical momentum, people from former African colonies, like people in Asia, begun their irreversible demand for independence of their countries.

Furthermore, when the United Nations was established in 1945, one of its principles was to promote "equal rights and self-determination of peoples" – a motivation that urged black Africans to free themselves from European colonial oppression through colonial independence struggles. With regard to the above comments made in the House of Commons, Winnick was not explicit if by Mugabe's friends, he was referring to the members of ZANU-PF or just personal friends of Mugabe. It is hard to fathom how any decent British person, who in one way or another had helped the people of Africa as well as people of Zimbabwe in good faith and with no obscure colonial interests in the continent, could go to the British House of Parliament to ask such an impertinent question, and, consequently, receive the praise of a British Prime Minister. He asked: "if a Commonwealth country that has abolished the rule of law and replaced it with outright violence were allowed to remain in the Commonwealth without any suspension, what would be the point of the Commonwealth?" – but one would ask him this: if a Prime Minister of a Commonwealth country, who pompously took his country to an illegal war in Iraq without listening to the majority of Commonwealth countries, especially to those in Africa, for example, South Africa, Nigeria and Zimbabwe, what would be the point of a Commonwealth community?

However, that member should also recall the following: anyone who has taken the trouble to look critically at documents related to Zimbabwe's history, particularly documents after the Second World War, would have noticed that whatever language was used in favour of the black Zimbabweans, Number 10 Downing Street and Westminster's ultimate goal was to avoid British white stock fleeing from Zimbabwe to the United Kingdom. In addition, the mainstream political anxiety amongst British politicians was that the United Kingdom could not afford the Kremlin to take control over Zimbabwe, as

was the case of the Portuguese former African colonies of Mozambique and
Angola. It is well known that British governments had encouraged white mi-
gration to Southern Rhodesia, particularly in years subsequent of the Second
World War, when many demobilised British soldiers from the war were encouraged to join hundreds of thousands of white settlers who had already
been in Rhodesia. These British people did not go to Zimbabwe in the sixties
or seventies to teach the superior virtues of European civilisation or look for
work opportunities, but to dispossess black Zimbabweans of their land and
live in a capitalist-bourgeoisie-aristocratic fashion, off the cheap labour, and
sometimes forced black African labour.

The UDI or the hijacking of Zimbabwe's independence by Ian Smith
amid African liberation momentum supported by the former Soviet Union
and China was seen by many in Westminster as Smith's political blunder,
which could lead to the loss of Zimbabwe's colony to the communist block.
These political manoeuvres could, therefore, undermine the British systematic control of that part of Africa through a commonwealth project. Winnick's
boasted claim suggests that Labour members campaigned in favour of black
majority rule in Zimbabwe. Indeed, that is true because Britain had a scheme
for the historical and political circumstances of those days, with a slight objective to maintain an imperial and neo-colonial absolute systematic control
over Southern Rhodesia, even after it was granted its independence.

Many people would still ask themselves why Ian Smith ignored serious
warnings from Harold Wilson, leader of the Labour Government, and proceeded with his plan of unilateral independence. There is a relevant historical
and political explanation for that. Smith maintained a tactical position for
two important reasons:

1. In his mind, Smith had all his political equations done – he was well
   aware and encouraged by the fact that he had support from some British
   politicians and the public. Britain would not attempt to take any military
   action against his illegal white regime which would involve British troops
   shamefully fighting their "kith and kin" in Africa. He contemplated that
   any British government which took such military action would be condemned by Britain, leading to a serious disruption for British society. In
   addition, any British government was also careful that taking any military action against Smith (in newly independent African countries of the
   sixties) would historically be a blunder, and politically would be a disaster
   for Westminster and the country as a whole.

2. Indeed, in view of this, even though Smith rejected the majority rule

through the principle of "one man – one vote", and defied the British Parliament as the sole institution holding the right to grant independence to any of its colonies, Britain felt that it could not act militantly against its white "kith and kin" in favour of the black Zimbabwean majority. Hence, deliberately, Britain allowed the illegal regime of Ian Smith to become independent on its own terms; subsequently, it turned a blind eye to a 15-year systematic black African bloodbath by the white racist anti-majority regime led by Ian Smith. Smith was secure, and Britain was also well aware that, on the one hand, if the minority white rulers were attacked, the then South Africa apartheid and Portuguese colonists in Mozambique and Angola would eventually come to their rescue. On the other hand, Smith, a victorious and relaxed white African, realised that Britain itself could not afford to lose Southern Rhodesia to the Kremlin; therefore, in such circumstances, whites from Britain would eventually be forced to intervene in an unprecedented expensive war in a black continent. Ian Smith and his coterie of whites' anti-majority rule had calculated all this.

Furthermore, faced with this dilemma, Britain had to play a cautious role in dealing with the Southern Rhodesian crisis, and used all political and magnanimous diplomatic language that would appease black Zimbabweans, particularly Zimbabwean revolutionary freedom fighters.

This was something that Portuguese colonists failed to do with their giant and former rich African colonies of Angola and Mozambique, and, even by the earlier seventies, when the Portuguese war in Africa was already consuming near 50% of the Portuguese budget and ignoring the decisive and irreversible African revolutionary struggle for the total independence of their continent.

Winnick **must** be reminded once and for all that Westminster's appeasing language continued even after black majority rule commenced in 1980. Winnick's political language strongly suggests that when Zimbabwe became independent, all honours, decorations and privileges bestowed on President Robert Mugabe by the United Kingdom were a reward to corrupt the President. This did not work with the Zimbabwean veteran of liberation struggle – Mugabe did not forget nor did he retreat from what he really fought for during their "chimurenga", **the land!**

As stated earlier in this chapter, with the help of the former Soviet Union block (the Soviet-led world communism expansion that was ready to respond to African emergency calls during Africa's colonial liberation struggle); China's involvement in African colonial liberation struggle; Yugoslavia's help to African liberation movements under Marshal Broz Tito; and between 1960 and 1990, the emerging African liberation movements, with strong anti-colonial manifestation and well supported by nationalism and communist ideology were unstoppable to freeing Africa from Western colonialism. In Africa and Asia, the independence movement acquired its momentum during and after the Second World War, when it became visible that the European colonial powers were weakened as a result of the war. Between 1960 and 1990, in Africa and Asia, successful independence movements emerged from one territory to another. This human historical process was influenced by the fact that colonised people around the globe realised that imperialism and colonialism were not virtuous entities and they could be resisted, and eventually defeated – this belief was once again reaffirmed after the Commonwealth Heads of Government Meeting (CHOGM) in Abuja, Nigeria, between December 5 and 8, 2003, when, Thabo Mbeki the South African President reiterated that he would resist "regime change" in Zimbabwe, meaning simply that he would resist imperialism and neo-colonialism in Africa.

After enduring more than 40 years of American embargo, Fidel Castro, the Cuban leader, has proved that imperialism can be well resisted. Africa's resistance to those evils had the support of the former Soviet Union and China after the Second World War, as both countries supported decolonisation around the world, while the USA regarded their initiative and communist ideological expansion as a threat to liberal world society.

The Soviet Union and China played a key role in the success of liberation movements around the world by providing all the necessary assistance that was needed. Also, constant pressures were mounting in the United Nations on total decolonisation of Africa by new African independent states, and supported by many other nations of the Third World that joined the United Nations since 1947, for example, India had forced Britain to rethink how it should resolve the conflicting situation in Southern Rhodesia and keep its commonwealth together.

Although it appears that many people in Britain believe that Ian Smith conceded to majority rule because of Western economic sanctions or through a British campaign against white minority rule, in fact it was because of a decisive African revolutionary struggle against Western colonial occupation. The independence of Rhodesia's neighbouring Mozambique and Angola from Portugal, and the engagement of the former Soviet Union and the presence of Cubans in Angola brought a fear not only to Ian Smith, but also to South African apartheid authorities as well as Britain and the USA. To prevent Soviets and Cubans from becoming directly involved with Zimbabwean revolutionary fighters, who had already been operating from Zambia under the leadership of Joshua Nkomo and from Mozambique under the leadership of Robert Mugabe, Smith was forced to negotiate a settlement that eventually led to a black majority rule in Zimbabwe.

Combining all the above factors, and avoiding British sanctions against its "kith and kin" to become perpetual, in 1979, the new Conservative Government under Mrs Thatcher had forced the white minority in Rhodesia to accept black majority rule – therefore, leading to the 1979 Lancaster House Agreement – a constitutional arrangement that led Zimbabwe to independence in 1980. With some constraints incorporated in the new London's Zimbabwean constitution, the concessions that were made by the black Zimbabwean fighters to see their aspirations of a long colonial liberation struggle materialised, had led to more successful negotiations than many other proposals made by previous British governments. In 1980, independence from Britain was granted to the colonial territory of Southern Rhodesia in Africa, which was then renamed 'Zimbabwe' – after the ancient stone ruins of Great Zimbabwe.

If we look back at he fifties and sixties when the liberation movements emerged in Africa with the inevitable help of the communist block, much effort and financial investment or financial offers were made available in occident to Africa in order to prevent this communist-expanding influence in the countries under occident, neo-colonial control in the continent, as the USA did under Marshall Plan immediately after the end of the Second World War. There was a threat that the Soviet Union and China might help liberation movements, and many former Western colonial powers in occident anticipated a form of decolonisation, which in some ways was regarded as neo-colonialism, and kept both military and economic influences in their former colonies.

3. MY CRITICISM OF THE RIGHT HONOURABLE MICHAEL ANCRAM, CONSERVATIVE MP FOR DEVIZES AND FORMER SHADOW SECRETARY FOR FOREIGN AFFAIRS.

"To remain a great nation or to become one, you must colonise". Statement made by Leon Gambetta, a French Statesman. (James Joll - 1973 - Europe since 1870 – Pg. 81).

Precluding Africans' genuine views on their continental affairs has been one of the causes of political contention between Africa and the West. The disrespectful comments made by Michael Ancram in the Sky News programme at the end of January 2005 are deeply offending to Africans. He vehemently demanded further EU sanctions to be imposed on selected ZANU-PF members on the basis of lack of freedom of press and human rights violations in Zimbabwe. The trouble with those at Westminster who advocate sanctions and "regime change" in Zimbabwe is that they do not concentrate on the factual causes of the bitterness between Westminster and Harare. The impression conveyed is reminiscent of the past: Western imperialists still have their dirty hands on the African continent. This persistent abysmal failure in the West creates some kind of circumspection among African leaders and leaves fair-minded people in Africa without any other alternative than to continue to generate strong African solidarity with the aim of resisting what Robert Mugabe describes as "born-again" in the continent.

The Rit Hon Michael Ancram is a member founder of 2005 Henry Jackson Society, which the main objective is to export the values of Western liberal democracy across the world, and if need be to impose it on other nations through military intervention. Although he has always envisaged a "resolute action" leading to the invasion of weaker nation of Zimbabwe, however, in relation to Iraq he eventually came to realise the cost of this foolish and irrational approach. As the result, frightened of possible civil war in Iraq, and writing in the *Daily Mail* in April 2006, the Conservative hardliner and advocate of British interventionist policy appealed for British troops to withdraw from Iraq immediately. In his own words, he stated: "It is time now for us to get out of Iraq with dignity and honour while we still can." Ancram's call for British troops to pull out of Iraq cannot please many aggressive MPs from both political parties, Labour and Conservative, who insist that whatever the situation and cost of lives in Iraq, British troops must stay until they had "finished the job" – benevolent job of restoring liberal democracy in Iraq as Condoleezza Rice lectured British people and the entire world during her recent visit to Britain.

British politicians do not invoke concerns for liberal democracy and human rights in countries where democracy and human rights are not observed as long as the political objectives of those countries favour Western economic and strategic interests. In Africa, perhaps apart of South Africa, I can see no other country to have held a general election with no irregularities and accusations of fraud. The US and the UK do not call for "regime change" in African countries where their economic investments are untouchable. Saudi Arabia has been friend to the US and the UK, despite that there has been no general election there, and this country has been known by the West to have an oppressive regime, particularly, the abusive way that the regime treats women.

The end of empires and decolonisation did not really mean the end of domination of the weaker countries by the stronger ones, as many ordinary people in the West might have believed. The powerful countries of the West have continued with their deliberate policy to subjugate the weaker states and keep them economically dependent and beggars to the West. This has been a long-term problem, and it is exactly what the G7 or G8 has been doing year by year since the Berlin G4 (The UK, Germany, France and Portugal) major European states that partitioned Africa during the 1884–1885 Berlin Conference on Africa. The European Imperial Conference lasted until February 26, 1885 and after a 3-month-period of vehement negotiations over European imperialist expansion and the establishment of boundaries in the interior of the African continent. Finally, the most powerful countries partitioned Africa between themselves. Moreover, after the remarkable surge of European imperialism, which divided Africa regardless of cultural and linguistic boundaries (already established by the indigenous African people), this prerogative was then followed by the European capitalist quick move that led to a massive and ravishing exploitation of Africa's natural resources and left a legacy of inequality, resulting from European capitalist greed, which is still the basis for the suspicious and contentious relations between Africa and the West.

The involvement of the north in the Third World never meant just humanitarian purpose sought to help Africans find efficient solutions to their flood of social and economic problems, but to pursue its own interests. In this context, far from helping the endless suffering of African people, as Ancram tries to disseminate, richer nations, in contrast, have been more interested in huge profit-making from Africa's enormous natural resources. And as it is well documented, the development of imperialism and colonialism has, for a long time, divided the world between stronger and weaker nations or north and south, as it is sometimes called. As a result, a certain fear or suspicious relationship has developed between these two opposite sides. On the one hand, the historical fear of continuing under the dominating manipulation of stronger and potent imperialist countries has been patent in the mind of the authorities of weaker states. On the other hand, the stronger imperialist powers have also maintained their fear or suspicion of the weaker states gaining power and control of their own destinies. This has long been a great cause of concern for the imperial powers in the West, particularly the fear of possible acts of revenge from their past victims of oppression and ordeals.

Asia has been developing at a pace that the West has been unable to restrain or control. Furthermore, there is a view that Western democracy will not deter the powerful emerging Chinese's 21st-century world economy, and, as a result the US and EU will gradually become less significant to the rest of the world, in spite of their strong democratic system. The US and the EU

know very well that Central and South America do not possess sufficient
natural resources needed for Western industries. Africa has been the only
continent left where the Western imperial powers still find it easier to control,
manipulate, divide and exploit. Permanent Western control of the black continent has not only over-prevented its economic development and growth,
but in many other invisible ways, Africans could not vouch for their own
history by what they know to be Africa's past, because they are prevented by
globalisation to validate and promote their identity, traditions and cultures
throughout the Western World.

It is therefore important for British politicians to publicly accept that the
political future of Zimbabwe as a sovereign nation has to be decided solely
by Zimbabwean people themselves. In Africa, it is unacceptable to see Britain
alongside its natural and historical allies in the Commonwealth, adopting
draconian policies aimed at isolating President Mugabe's Government at international level, particularly from the European Union and the US. Britain's
vicious approach to Zimbabwe does not do any good for the people of
Zimbabwe: instead, it goes on fuelling strong division between Zimbabweans
to a point of making one group of people turn against the duly elected
Zimbabwean Government. While some aggressive politicians at Westminster
such as Ancram, recklessly stimulate division in Zimbabwe with the intention
to find a bogus excuse for military intervention, however, President Mbeki
and many other African leaders have been adopting a policy which is aimed
at bringing together all people of Zimbabwe through national reconciliation,
as the only way to avoid more bloodshed in the African continent.

Moreover, Mr. Ancram should know better than many Africans themselves that land has been a central issue. At the "1979-Lancaster House
conference" the constitutional and diplomatic discussions that culminated
in Zimbabwe's Independence in 1980 were influenced by Britain to protect
white settlers' land and British economic interests in Zimbabwe. The current
controversial political and diplomatic crises between both sovereign states,
Zimbabwe and Britain cannot be fully understood without an attempt to
bring the land question to the core of the discussion. It is also useful to recall
that the period between 1900 and 1980 was important in the history of colonialism in Zimbabwe – a particular period where successive British colonial
regimes or governments had systematically dispossessed Africans of the natural land inherited from their forefathers, through deliberate action and inaction that was aimed at transferring land and livestock from indigenous black
Zimbabweans to white settlers. Land reform has been central and one of the
key issues behind Zimbabwe's current political situation, which has its roots
deep in colonial history. Therefore, when the land issue arises, it cannot and

should not be confusing to Michael Ancram and others because President Mugabe never concealed his stance. In his own words, he made it very clear:

> When I went to prison and I spent all those years in exile during our struggle, I did it to get our land back – and that is precisely what the war veterans are doing. I mustn't be seen as negating myself.

President Mugabe is determined to pursue the land issue to his last day, as notable Zimbabweans did the same for him previously. ZANU-PF Website recalls this:

> **"Land should be given to its rightful owners"-Chirimanyemba-** John Taviringana Chirimanyemba, a centurion who witnessed whites when they invaded, conquered and seized land in Zimbabwe and later emerged as an advocate of the liberation movement, 'advancing the idea of resisting the unjust political, economic and social subjection has one wish before he dies, to see land given back to its rightful owners.

It is crystal clear and a matter of principle that the land redistribution programme was inevitable to correct the imbalances in land ownership rooted in the Zimbabwe colonial era. It has also been pointed out by many people inside and outside of Zimbabwe that the current Government has made some mistakes of judgement as to whom the land should be given. Zimbabwean Government officials have openly recognised this misjudgement too. Redistribution of land to some black Zimbabweans with no previous link or experience of agricultural farming has been one of the factors leading to food shortages in Zimbabwe. This mistake has been recognised by official members within the Government. But, British politicians also should take account the reports from the 2003 IMF (International Monetary Fund), 12002 USDA (United States Department of Agriculture) and the 2004 UN, explaining that the devastating food shortages since 2000 were largely to be blamed on the severe drought. In 2003, Mr Ismaila Usman, IMF's Executive Director for Zimbabwe, asserted that the drought was the worst in 50 years, and appealed to the IMF to give Zimbabwe another chance.

Also, diseases were among the flood of problems facing Africans, such as the exterminating HIV/AIDS which is regarded as a serious obstacle that affects African labour population, and hence impairs African economic development and prosperity.

In addition, land conflict occurs not only in Zimbabwe, as might appear to many Westerners. In fact, some people in Britain and in the rest of the West might be unaware of the land-issue in Namibia simply because the Namibian Government has been trying hard to protect the white settler farmers, whose lands are being reclaimed by their original and natural owners, the indigenous black people. Namibia has been with its land problems too, and, it could be only a matter of time before land-issue in Namibia gets out of the Namibian Government control, where, long before the country's independence, commercial farming was monopolised by the minority white farming population. Western governments have been aware of it, particularly Germany as the first former colonial power, which it is said was reluctant to release the fund needed to prevent what is actually happening in Zimbabwe. Land reform in Namibia has already been in the spotlight and has become a central political question. The Namibian Government has already pledged to its people that it would take a radical move to bring equity into land ownership as soon as possible through a process of government expropriation. As a matter of fact, addressing the nation in a special national live TV coverage on the land question, in February 25, 2004, on behalf of his government, the Namibian Prime Minister, Theo-Ben Gurirab stated:

Tonight I come before you to address you on the Government's efforts to accelerate the land reform process in Namibia.

It will be recalled that the land possession pattern in our country
has been designed by colonialism to benefit a small group of minority settlers, at the expense of the majority.
Therefore, the problem of land ownership was indeed central to
the struggle for national independence. Today, generations after the
systematic dispossession, our young nation still struggles to bring
about balance and undo the effects of the unjust land distribution.
With full recognition of the history of colonial oppression, apartheid and land dispossession, the founding fathers and mothers
of the Namibian Constitution decided on a new Chapter for the
Namibian nation, built on national unity and reconciliation...
Over the years, the Government has come to realise that the
'Willing-Seller/Willing-Buyer' approach would not be able to keep
up with the high public demand for agricultural land...

For many Africans, a ban on ZANU-PF President and its members as well as on any African leader from travelling to Western Europe has been regarded as a joke. This in turn suggests that world leaders from the Third World come to the Western Europe's paradise to show off rather than for official business. It is widely argued amongst Africans that Britain, the US, the EU and the white commonwealth governments which impose travel bans, economic sanctions, and motivate the world for a total isolation of ZANU-PF members, do not constitute the "wider international community". On April 27, 2004, President Robert Mugabe was among the 20 African leaders officially invited to South Africa's celebration which marked the country's 10th anniversary of freedom and democracy and the pledge of President Thabo Mbeki for a second term in office. A very warm and happy noisy welcome was given to President Robert Mugabe by dignitaries and politicians from across the continent. These are African dignitaries who have been less informed of Zimbabwe's problems than him. Moreover, his views might tend to indicate that those African dignitaries, who rose to their feet to applaud President Mugabe, should disregard any recognition of the President's role and contribution to Africa's struggle for its complete liberation from colonialism and apartheid. From the language used in British political society against Mugabe, it is clear that Ancram cannot take comfort in any event where African leaders are supportive of Mugabe. He regards those African dignitaries as foul black people who had behaved immorally in relation to the suffering of the Zimbabwean people, for whom he has been more concerned than Africans themselves. Furthermore, Mugabe's presence at this auspicious event prevented Mr. Blair from attending, an immature gesture that suggests to Africans that the South African Government does not understand the current crisis in Zimbabwe, as both parties, Labour and Conservative do, and that Mugabe should also be banned from travelling to South Africa. In that important national event, people of South Africa confirmed their recognition of the current South African Government's performance in the management of the economy and social policy of South Africa. However, they also expected that their government would do more as at the same time, they felt happy with the foreign policy, especially, South Africa's standing to a unilateral US–UK-led illegal war in Iraq.

It is also important to note that the British media tries to undermine the efforts of the majority young South African Government because of the approach taken by President Mbeki, an African veteran in international politics who has an acknowledged understanding of the current problems in Zimbabwe. In the run-up to the last election in South Africa the British media emphasizes the neglect and deterioration of the country; a rise in unemployment, rise in crime, lack of adequate housing provision for black people, poverty still alarming, failure in tackling HIV/AIDS, and so forth. This has been intentional British media propaganda in support of a vicious and aggressive British foreign policy towards Africa. Propaganda intended to discredit and foment division which could rally South African people against President Thabo Mbeki and his Government for being fair to the political situation in Zimbabwe, through resisting British neo-colonial ambitions in Zimbabwe, and by devoting much effort to a peaceful solution that could unite people of that African independent and sovereign country.

Fair-minded people across the world always express their gratitude and appreciation to people who campaign for human understanding. What Africans have been looking for is a close human understanding, and it is regrettable in these circumstances that efforts in that direction have been deeply undermined by Western disparagement of Africans. Thabo Mbeki's effort to secure a peaceful solution in Zimbabwe has been disregarded by many British politicians, and in its place, a doctrine of "regime change" has been invoked in London by the champion of Africa's cause, Mr. Tony Blair. Africans cannot achieve a true human understanding with the old Western mentality or disrespectful interference in the continent, because they believe in their own traditional and cultural values in resolving their problems and on African people's own terms.

The right of Africans to resist any form of neo-colonialism has also been vilified by vaunted accusations of lack of democracy and respect for human rights. These are accusations aimed at deflecting African people's attention to the crucial causes resulting to a flood of problems affecting the continent. For the West, lack of democracy and human rights are core issues when Africans raise their voices to say that enough is enough, and form a resistance to demand the respect and dignity of African people as human beings; when Africans press for free and fair economic trade; when Africans fight to preserve their natural rights rather than giving up their ancestral land, and so forth. Hence, once again, it is apt to Ancram appreciate that Africans have endured a struggle and that there are individuals on this planet who do not understand or ignore the maxim of Africans: "*love our land and love us too*".

The British theory or assumption that land redistribution to black Zimbabweans would lead to a permanent food shortage in Zimbabwe is a reflection on the excuse of West European domination since the period of colonialism. The assumption being that people in Africa would remain incapable and lack intellectual thinking to resolve their own social and economic problems, therefore, Africa has to remain a dependent on the West's alms. Michael Ancram's perspective of food shortage in Zimbabwe is categorically refuted through the fact that for many years, indigenous Zimbabweans have been the backbone of agricultural production even in white-owned commercial farms. It is a complete misrepresentation to consider that if even an international subsidy be made available to black farmers as has been made available to Western farmers, the return of land to their original owners would anyway mean a shortage of agricultural produces in Zimbabwe. Furthermore, it is well known in Africa that former colonists would always be very glad to hear Africans repeatedly saying or crying that under English colonists "we had enough cheaper jobs and a breadbasket; under French colonists we had enough medicine and clothing; under Portuguese colonists we had enough food and red wine and so forth – and since they all left, we have been suffering than ever before". If my memory is accurate, in a Sky News TV programme, Michael Ancram stated in his own words: *"when we left [Zimbabwe] there was enough food..."*, and in his response to my letter, he has reinforced this view by stating: *"Zimbabwe was, for many years, the breadbasket of Africa producing enough food not simply to feed itself but to feed much of the continent."*. This is one kind of Western contemptuous behaviours at concerns Africans and being at the centre of suspicious relations between the West and Africa. It is deeply offending to Africans when someone from New Zealand expresses publicly in these disdaining words: *"Africa will not deal with Zimbabwe, as all the current leaders of most Southern African nations are ex terrorists who by expelled the white experts who kept the nations functioning. A bitter truth."* (Chris Dunbar, New Zealand)

Ancram did not tell the public who produced that breadbasket, the individuals who made exorbitant profits from it nor the banks into which this exorbitant profit was channelled. Ancram must be reminded that rapid industrialisation of Europe has led to the occupation of other people's lands and was a pursuit of Western nations' self-economic interests. Neither Europe's industrialisation or globalisation was intended for social and economic prosperity of local populations, but primarily to further the standard of living of the valued people in the civilised Western nations of Europe. In his book, 'The no-nonsense guide to globalization, 2001, Wayne Ellwood appears right to state that globalization only can help as positive force for change if we as human being come to recognize the common thread of humanity that ties us together. It appears right to support the idea of universality, which consists of the belief that man is able to make the world a better place for all, by both improving technology and developing scientific research in a universal belief that we live in a world in which we are surrounded by enormous wealth and opportunity, which should be shared equitably; consequently, every human being should be better off in a wonderful world. Unfortunately, all this has not yet been achieved because of human greed and the Western disrespectful approach to other races. Western greed makes the West a better place through massive exploitation of Africa's natural resources, bribes and the promotion of corruption which have been among the most crucial causes of Africa's tragedies. If human ambitions were simply not self-centred around their own interests, but were more wisely directed to the human social good it might be possible, for people to achieve a uniform standard of living in the entire world now. It is therefore appreciated the initiative taken by India, Brazil and South Africa to build on the strong unity of their nations and send signals to the richer nations, emphasising that dependence on them has become a thing of the past. This initiative is saluted by any country that wishes to become liberated from long-standing Western economic dependency. It is certain that sooner or later, many other Third World countries, including those in Africa will also join the enterprise.

It would be erroneous to put all the blame for African social and economic crises on Europeans. Therefore I must emphasised to the Right Honourable Member that although I do not intend to place all the blame for Africa's social and economic misfortune(s) on former Western colonial powers; however, it should not be ignored or regarded as a matter of less relevance that Africa has been deeply betrayed by its former European colonists. As a consequence of that legacy, Africa has continued to be betrayed by some of its own leaders, who also imitated the greed of European imperialists by pursuing their personal prestige, power, greed, and a transfer of huge amount of their national public money to Western bank accounts. In fact, they perpetuate their own fellow African citizens to unnecessary social suffering, far more than they experienced during the Western colonial period. But, overall, the Western greed has been one of the greatest causes for Africa's suffering. And to make sense of it, Lenin's approach to South–North relations was based on the idea that industrialised countries exploit poor countries, and, consequently, use profits from this exploitation to buy off their own working class. In addition, as the West advocates African economic development and prosperity, it has also introduces many problems that have since been devastating the continent. Let us now ask these questions: Who creates economic problems in Africa? Who brought wars to Africa? Who most benefits from economic cooperation between the West and Africa? Who are the major protectionists in the world? Who imposes economic sanctions and embargos to other states? I think the answers to these questions are obvious to many of us.

In his speech to the Action for Southern Africa seminar (ACTSA) on November 20, 1999, Peter Hain, then Foreign and Commonwealth Minister of State, delivered these generous words to appease ordinary Africans:

> There should be full transparency. The oil companies who work
> in Angola, like BP-Amoco [British Oil Company], Elf, Total and
> Exxon and the diamond traders like de Beers, should be open

with the international community and the international financial institutions so that it is clear these revenues are not siphoned off but are invested in the country. I want the oil companies and the governments of Britain, the USA and France to cooperate together, not seek a competitive advantage; full transparency is in our joint interests because it will help to create a more peaceful, stable Angola and a more peaceful, stable Africa too.

These passionate words have been left in the annotations filed somewhere in Whitehall. These are words that cannot be bought by Africans because of the fact that they are not a method of redressing the illness of African economies and are such that they are not focused on the question of full transparency and the fight on corruption. But these words should also focus on how those international financial institutions which agree to the short-term loans investment in Africa at exorbitant interest rates, and to the intricate workings of the Western national governments, which assist such business arrangements and how much responsibilities these governments can accept. Paradoxically, it is because of that, while Western governments require full transparency of Africa's economies, many ordinary Africans complain to the very same Western governments that there has been a huge amount of Africa's money in Western banks. This is money (transferred by some African elites) that could be used to alleviate some of the social problems in many African countries. Instead, this money has been producing interest rates, and, perhaps the profits serve as social welfare provision for people in the West.

Moreover, it is not the aim of this book to lecture British politicians on international norms and democratic values. The ultimate people to decide on "regime change" in Zimbabwe are Zimbabweans themselves, whatever corrosive notions they may have about President Robert Mugabe. Zimbabweans will make their decisions through the polls. Although politicians at Westminster have maliciously complained about Zimbabwe's Parliamentary elections held on March 31, 2005, these elections have been endorsed by most African countries as being free and fair. The Southern African Development Community (SADC) said the vote reflected the will of the Zimbabwean people despite other monitors saying that it was neither free nor fair. President Thabo Mbeki added by saying that Zimbabwe was the only country so far to have altered its electoral laws in response to the SADC protocols, while his neighbour Namibia, and in the voice of the former President Mr Sam Nujoma, emphasised this:

I think the situation there in Zimbabwe is moving now towards a goal that the government of Zimbabwe has worked out for the

common benefit of all the people of Zimbabwe. There is really no
serious problem there, no problem there…

Finally, this development has to be regarded as a good starting point in
the further development of democracy in Zimbabwe. However, many British
politicians at Number 10 Downing Street and Westminster are still not satisfied. Michael Ancram, a Conservative MP who lacks the ability and charisma
to run his own party or even stand for its leadership contest, and who has
disappeared from the Shadow Cabinet list still pursues an interventionist and
neo-colonialist policy in Africa – his end-goal in Africa is to see President
Robert Mugabe out of power in favour of British economic interests in
Zimbabwe. I do not foresee any future success in Michael Ancram's political
career, hence, the sooner he retires to establish his own charitable organisation
the better. Establishing charities has now become a new fashion for retired
Western politicians and celebrities.

4. MY CRITICISM OF MR ANDREW HOPKINSON AT THE FOREIGN AND COMMONWEALTH OFFICE, SOUTHERN AFRICA DEPARTMENT.

On January 19, 2004 I wrote to Mr Chris Mullin, British Minister
for Africa, expressing my indignation about the British foreign policy towards Africa. In his replying letter dated February 2, 2004, on behalf of Mr
Mullin, Mr Andrew Hopkinson of the Foreign and Commonwealth Office,
at Southern Africa Department, dismissed the South African President Thabo
Mbeki's statement that the current Zimbabwean's land crisis has been caused
by the UK and other Western powers by breaking their promises to fund
peaceful land redistribution in Zimbabwe. Mbeki is an African veteran politician who, among many like Nelson Mandela, had fought for Africa's cause
and had contributed to unusual national reconciliation in South Africa, and
continues to be an exemplar African leader who imparts to other African
nations the values of democracy and national reconciliation, as he has been
doing with Zimbabwe's political situation and the Democratic Republic of
Congo's social and political crises.

Not focusing much on President Mbeki, it is important to remind Mr
Hopkinson that at the Abuja meeting, African leaders agreed by consensus to the four GIANTS' pre-determined decision to continue indefinitely
Zimbabwe's suspension from the Commonwealth. This was because of the
habitual fear of the weaker nations to prevent Western economic sanctions
and isolation, which have since been one of the most powerful tools of dominion and control of African people's own destinies. However, this book

does not mean to blame those African leaders, because they are fully aware of this long-standing Western game that will persist as long as Africans will need Western financial aid. And in times of despair, whether it is conditional or it comes from an evil, any financial aid will be welcomed in Africa. Many African countries await assistance from the G7, and politicians from G7 countries are conscious of the fact that Africans have no other choice but to accept Blair's financial aid to urgently tackle the monstrous and exterminating HIV/AIDS crisis that has been ravaging the continent. HIV/AIDS has also condemned African people to continue to be more dependent on the West's alms than ever before. They are the beggars of money and cheap retroviral drugs from their past oppressors and torturers – compounding factors that diminish their dignity and respect as a race created by the same God. African leaders desperately need money from the richest civilised nations to save the lives of those who can still be saved, especially children and the African labour force that Africa's economic development and prosperity rely on. Money is needed for educational projects to prevent and slow the rapid spread of disease. One example on how people in total despair would accept any aid, wherever it comes from, is the established fact that during the eighties, some Angolan rebels of the National Union for Total Independence of Angola (UNITA) defended their military cooperation with the then worldwide detested 'regime of apartheid' in South Africa by rhetorically questioning this:

> When our liberation movement, UNITA (National Union for the Total Independence of Angola) was on the verge of extinction face to a massive Cuban troops advance, a foreign occupation force of our land, Angola, and therefore, an evil [South African troops under Apartheid] came in our rescue, had we rejected their help? And they themselves gave the answer to this, "Certainly not".

It is obvious that people who are desperate to survive will accept any help from whence it comes. This is exactly what is happening with African countries. Some civilised Western governments deliberately seize this African tragedy as an opportunity to perpetuate African people into their subservient. By accepting aid, Africans are accepting domination or control of their own development plans, because aid to Africa has been conditioned. For some times this has been regarded as a form of corruption of the superpowers in recruiting countries to merge with them and as a continued form of penetration, where interests and strategic positions have to be maintained with no regard to the sovereignty and self-determination of weaker nations.

Again, in another letter to me, Hopkinson brought to my attention the

£62 million that was made available by the British Government to Zimbabwe in the form of aid since 2001. When I checked with the Zimbabwe High Commission in London on the amount referred by Hopkinson, I found that since 2001, the £62 million was paid in the form of reimbursement for which the Zimbabwean Government had to spend first and present credible and accurate receipts to be reimbursed, and the sum of £3 million out of this £62 million has remained undelivered. In reality, this is small money and nowhere near the amount that the current US Government under Bush has already spent in Iraq on accomplishments such as rewarding those who have provided information leading to the capture of the most wanted former Iraqi leaders, including Saddam Hussein. Indeed, not even near the amount of money made available to the CIA and the US Special Forces since September 11 to reward those who provide reliable information leading to the capture of terrorists. And, as a matter of fact, a paragraph in the book *'Bush at War'* by Bob Woodward reveals:

In one of USA president's daily intelligence briefings, at 8 am of September 12, 2003, Tenet, CIA Director briefed Bush on Al-Qaeda by making the president know that an expanded cover plan in Afghanistan had been in the works for months, an even more expanded plan would be presented for approval, and it would be expensive, very expensive. Though Tenet did not use a figure, but it was estimated to approach $1 billion dollars".

George W Bush, President of the richest nation in the world, said this to Tenet: *"whatever it takes"*. Obviously, he meant that any sum of money would be made available for the CIA in this respect.

Many of us know that the Blair Government has been spending billions of pounds of British taxpayers' money on the war in Iraq to kill thousands of innocent Iraqi children, but the very same Government has failed to deliver money needed in Zimbabwe to save the lives of thousands of Zimbabwean children from starvation that Westminster claims to be taking place in Zimbabwe.

Finally, it should be emphasised that some information on Zimbabwe's general situation has been exaggerated as was the case with Iraq. And, in point of fact, I referred Hopinkson to *The Guardian* (newspaper) – Friday 16, 2004 – Front page – which states:

UK charities exaggerated Africa crisis, says report - Some of Britain's leading international charities who tried to help southern Africa avoid a food crisis in 2002-03 overstated the seriousness of the situation to the public... But together they made many mistakes, including not fully appreciating the links between food crisis and HIV/AIDS - British Red Cross knew there were no starving millions in Zimbabwe...

5. MY CRITICISM OF MR JOHN REDWOOD AND MR TIM YEO, BOTH CONSERVATIVE MPs.

At the David Dimbleby's BBC TV Question Time programme held June 9, 2005, John Redwood disingenuously advocated the 'no' aid to undemocratic and corrupt African Governments without explaining to his audience the origin of Africa's corruption, and who has created and supported African dictators during the Cold War. On the Adam Boulton 2005 June Sunday Sky News programme, Tim Yeo appeared to lecture the world that "we cannot make poverty history until we make corruption and good governance in Africa a history", without looking at the two-way corruption between Western and African actors. However, the following criticism was also emphasised in a letter I addressed to Mr. Tim Yeo, on July 5, 2005.

We cannot lecture or address the issue of corruption in Africa without first explaining or addressing the roots of corruption itself. We cannot talk about Africa's corruption without looking at the two-way corruption between Western and African actors. Consideration how the political economy of imperialism works, it is obvious who are the most fortunate in economic cooperation between the West and Africa – we also know who imposes economic sanctions and embargoes on other states and why.

Redwood and Yeo seem to suggest that the universal principles of governance can be applied in Africa, despite the Western actors' complicity to Africa's corruption. In the contemporary context, the political economy of imperialism can only operate with the green light given by influential African local rulers who are also devoted to the pillage, corruption and repression of their own people, resulting in a setback to the development and prosperity that the West needs in Africa. It is obvious that the Western multinational companies which exploit Africa's main natural resources such as oil, the Western international financial institutions which arrange short-term loans at exorbitant profit rates and the Western national governments which assist such business have been working hand in hand and partly contributing to the grotesque poverty that prevails in Africa. It is also believed that huge amounts of money from Africa's export earnings have been kept in Western banks by corrupted Africans, while millions of people in Africa have been living in miserable social conditions, which British MPs are keen to tackle because of the present mounting and irreversible popular pressure over the richest and civilised Western governments.

Yeo and Redwood should ponder over a few relevant examples of Western complicity with regard to Africa's corruption. The author of a book called *Work, consumerism and the new poor,* by Zygmunt Bauman puts it right:

> ...And so the 'reserve army of labour' and the costs of its readiness for active service are now global, while all welfare provisions are state-bound and - like the state authority itself - local. The arms of the state are much too short to reach where it truly counts. To the expansion and security of capital the old-style state's assistance has become largely irrelevant. The local businessmen knowing only too well that to remain businessmen they better stop being local, need their prime ministers and foreign secretaries, mostly as their trade agents to introduce and endear them to the authorities of the targeted localities during their diplomatic voyages, and if need be to subsidize the trips.

In one of the *Global Witness* magazines, 'crude awakening, 1999, page 10, it is revealed:

> France's Elf oil company has for many years played the game of African politics not only to win control over coveted oil licences, but as an arm of French diplomacy and intelligence. It has always a dubious multinational company activities in Africa by mixing politics with corporate gain. President Jacques Chirac's visit to Angola [Southern Africa] in June 1998, was prompted, above all, by Elf's efforts at the time to secure as good a position as possible in the recent attribution of ultra-deep licences 31-33. Elf was eventually awarded operatorship of block 32. Although Elf is currently a private company, but the old political channels still run deep, and the company continues to use its expertise in African politics to gain access to markets such as Angola.

The Guardian, Thursday, June 2, 2005 – with a headline and sub-headline states:

> A rich country being stripped of its wealth" - "British firms among those to profit from energy bonanza in Equatorial Guinea". And then its first paragraph states: "It has a sad record of disease, brutality and corruption, and fewer inhabitants than

Sheffield. But Equatorial Guinea is one of the key targets of the West's new "scramble for Africa". So much so that a gang of British businessmen, including [prominent] Sir Mark Thatcher, were accused last year of financing an armed coup to get their hands on its wealth. The UK companies which are involved in the corrupt business are BG, formerly British Gas, now international Oil and gas trader. This company won't disclose price, and some proceeds alleged to go to regime officials; HSBC, based in London – it has been reluctant to disclose who gets oil cash; ECL Group, a small consultancy - it privately delivered confidential payments to educated Equatorial Guinea elite in the UK; INCAT Group, a construction firm based in Jersey - it has no accounts published; Logo Logistics - Guernsey, owned by Simon Mann who was has promised £7m by British investors - the deal was to overthrow the President of Equatorial Guinea, Obiang Nbguema and gain control of oil assets. And as you know, the coup plot which involved South African mercenaries has eventually failed". Finally, Guardian confirms that **"Profits from [Equatorial] Guinea's natural resources are bypassing the country.**

Corruption is occurring everywhere in the world. The difference is that European corruption is performed in a classic manner. Very recently, the British Ministry of Defence has been accused of a £2.5 million pay scam, dating back 3 years. It was reported that at least £2.5 m has been deviated towards expenses-and-pay scams involving about 650 'ghost soldiers'. Suspicion also emerged last January after troops were found to be spending considerable sums on cars, homes and holidays. Who are involved in these high profile national fraud operations?

Are we forgetting about Peter Mandelson's Hindu passport and homes' stories? David Blunkett and the nanny's residence permit? Are we forgetting about Blair's son offer of a job within the British Embassy in Washington?

On the subject of bad governance in Africa, I am compelled to sell to Tim Yeo and John Redwood the following story:

When I went to Cuba in the earlier 1980's, I discovered the Cuban social and economic organisation that gave me a clear perception and an awareness of bad governance in Africa. When I returned to Angola from Cuba in 1982, where I undertook 1-year's military training and Marxism-Leninism studies, I clandestinely happened to criticise bad governance in Africa. At that time, my criticism was based on the view that it was inconceivable that Cuba, as poor country in terms of natural resources, could have a well-organised welfare state system than many rich African nations in natural resources. The Cuban Government's huge investment in public health and education in particular, was impressive and was perhaps the envy of the rest of the world and the people in Latin America in particular. For example, because of hard military training in Cuba, I developed a hernia illness, which needed surgery, and was operated on immediately. I was not placed in a waiting list, which for instance, has been a worrying system within the British National Health Service.

Moreover, on bad governance in Africa, I want to recall to Tim Yeo my experience of former Zaire (currently, Democratic Republic of Congo). Portuguese colonial oppression forced my parents to escape from Angola to the neighbouring Congo/Kinshasa (which afterwards was renamed to Zaire and again to the current Democratic Republic of Congo), where we lived as refugees for a number of years since I was just 3 years old. We returned to Angola in 1975, when it gained its independence from Portugal. During 1960 and 1970, Zaire's economy appeared to perform well as inflation was low, people could manage well with their wages and most parents could afford for enough food, health costs and send their children to school. Combined with other issues of economic mismanagement and wars, since former Zaire was flooded with short Western loans (at exorbitant profit rates) for prestigious projects that did not benefit people at large; Western loans for Mobutu to sustain its one time the best armed forces in Africa and his Presidential special forces/security forces, eventually, the country found itself accumulated with debts that it could not repay and an economic decline to recover so far. When I left former Zaire in 1975, the country was already on the verge of social and economic collapse. When I last visited it in 1987, the social and economic conditions of its people were dreadful. Former Zaire seemed to have no functioning government; the head of State, late President Mobutu Sese Seko, a Kleptocrat-in-Chief, an African statesman misled by Western imperialism on how to exploit and repress his own people and a remarkable African dictator who owned his Congo/Kinshasa as Belgian King Leopold II owned it as a personal possession from 1885 to 1960; Mobutu, the autocrat who clung to power for 32 years with the support of the CIA, had already retreated from the capital city, Kinshasa, to his home village of Gbadolite, after retrieving all foreign currencies from the Zaire's banks, leaving behind him a chaos and anarchy not seen before. At that time, I visited a relative at Kinshasa's general hospital of Mama Yemo, named after Mobutu's mother 'Mama Yemo' hospital that was one time one of the African modern hospitals, had deteriorated beyond recognition. When I left the hospital I decided not to return there because of the appalling conditions of sanitation, corruption and lack of any sense of hospitality that prevailed there. Hospital management personnel and ordinary workers were not paid and they did not even know when their arrear payments were due. To sustain themselves and their families, hospital staff relied on corruption, illegal vending of hospital supplies and other kind of dishonesty practices within that health institution.

My comparison of Cuba with the African governments' performance on social and economic management, particularly my observation of the deterioration of Angola's economy and the suffering of millions of ordinary Angolans at that time, added to the reasons that eventually forced me to leave my country, Angola in 1989 and reside in the United Kingdom. But after living in the UK for some years, I was compelled to change my approach with regard to bad governance and corruption in Africa, because I concluded that much of Africa's economic decline and social misery were caused by the West during the Cold War, a period in which the West itself promoted and supported African dictators, who by proxy fought communism expansion; other contributing factors to poverty in Africa are the Western multinational greed, Western unfair trade system, the United States and United Kingdom unjustified economic sanctions against their detested regimes in Africa, such as the case of Zimbabwe, led by President Robert Mugabe, a Number 10 and Westminster implacable African enemy number 1, and so forth.

CONCLUSION

CONCLUSION

OVERALL, I would briefly conclude this book by first agreeing with all those who hold the view that the current British foreign policy under Labour, foreign policy manipulated by the current US administration has been at the centre of the malaise between the United Kingdom and the rest of world, particularly, the Third World. Looking back after nine years of Labour Government record in handling international affairs, Blair has mostly summed unpleasant, if not dreadful records, leading to many people across the UK and the world to discredit him as a good-nurtured world leader, but also, regard him not only as one of the most worst British Prime Ministers in the history of Britain, an international authoritarian and dictator who counts with support of elites from other side of Atlantic to achieve his great ambition of historical and international statesman by all dirty and vain means, including lies, baseless sanctions, threats and invasion of independent and sovereign weaker nations in the Third World on the humanitarian grounds and in the name of his God. Blair's perversity to pursue an imperialist old dream to maintain the US/UK's dominion over world weaker nations is no longer an option in the world we live in today and alas, it calls into question the democratic and nations' mutual respect principles upon which this Great nation should stand by. It is safe to call attention to the fact that Britain no longer has a major influence in the current world. And historically, although Britain did not attach a significant interest in the European Union development as France and Germany have done since its inception after the Second World War, however, it has now to follow the example of many West European nations and others, such as Russia, China and Japan, which have adopted and developed a friendly foreign policy in dealing with the Third World rather than imposing and threatening them with "regime change" and unjustified diplomatic and economic sanctions. It is also safe to recall that with fear of the former Soviet military intervention in the Suez conflict known as 'Suez Crisis'

131

(Egypt) and in 1957, forced (along with France) by Americans to abandon the Suez Canal, Britain saw the completion of the transfer of the global balance of power from traditional European powers to the United States and the former Soviet Union. This was a remarkable moment in the history when Britain begun to realise its decline of power and British Empire, and its major influence in any part of the world had been ever since diminished. These unpalatable historical events have left Britain with no country to play a major influence as the White House does with Israel in the Middle East. Therefore, when some politicians at Westminster foster the vain hope of their imperialist ambition of maintaining Zimbabwe under British influence or as Britain's Israel of Africa, without reflecting on the Africa's twenty-first century which has been characterized by revolutionary new ideas and realities, the South Africa led by a vigilant President Thabo Mbeki takes the lead in opposing Blair's imperialist "regime change" in Zimbabwe – and takes the lead in helping in the direction of peaceful political solutions through reconciliation and unification not only of the people of Zimbabwe, but of all African people on African terms. This is one of the main causes why the President has been viewed by some British politicians at Westminster as not doing things or not acting to British model.

The current malaise between Britain and Africa is sometimes exasperated by Blair, a British Premier who does not talk with those whose he himself describes as dictators, terrorists, evils and so forth. There is a little doubt that Blair is politically much more articulated than Bush, but, the US world military and economic lead require that Blair and many others within the British political community to take some more lectures on foreign policy from Bush. The disrespectful and arrogant negative depiction of other people is an approach that Westminster has imported from the US foreign policy, which, for instance, *if you are friend of our enemies, you therefore are our enemy too.* It also means that the enemy countries created by the US as a result of its own manipulating and imposing foreign policy, are automatically considered as enemy countries to Britain by Westminster and Number 10 Downing Street. This is a Western interpretation by those who believe that they are endowed with superior human explanations. This US/UK conception means, for example, when Blair and Bush label both Fidel Castro and Robert Mugabe as fascist dictators and their enemies, it simply implies that in the US/UK, Nelson Mandela has to be regarded as an enemy fascist dictator himself for the fact that he had invited both world leaders (as part of 140 invited world politicians and dignitaries) at his 1994 inaugural ceremony as South Africa's first black president after more than three centuries of white minority rule.

Moving on the current British bad foreign policy, many people across the country, including politicians at Westminster are too worried and strongly suspect that we still face the greatest chance of being killed or amputated by a massive terrorist bomb attacks in London, one time a peaceful city, because of the Britain's involvement in Iraq and partly because of the British Labour softer laws, which allow people to express any sort of language that may stimulate violence or act as they wish with no regard to established British laws. During the last Conservative party conference in Bournemouth, it was strongly pointed out that the Tories need to be tough on crime – tougher that Blair's Labour. But in my perspective, this assertion needs a careful consideration. There is a serious dilemma for British politicians to seek tougher laws if we ponder the following questions: how a reckless/aggressive British Prime Minister and his associates at Westminster, including David Davis, Conservative Shadow for Home Office, who disregard the international rule of law, the United Nations' international authority and contempt for the overwhelming international community's opinions – how can those who threaten and encourage the use of force to change regimes in sovereign and independent nations – change regimes that are not docile to the US/UK seek tougher laws over British public? Why is it that British tougher laws should not commence by punishing Tony Blair, who lied to the British people and took this country to the wrong war? Do the lives of innocent Iraqi people and British soldiers who have been dying as a result of a war based on Blair's lies matter?

However, in addressing his last party conference in Bournemouth, David Davis felt justified by emphasizing on the opportunities and prosperity that refugees/immigrants have been benefiting in the UK. In his own words, Davis stated: "opportunities and prosperity they wouldn't have enjoyed elsewhere." On this point, at least there is a credit for our Right Honourable David Davis. He is absolutely right to emphasize on the opportunities and prosperity that many immigrants enjoy in this country. And as a matter of principle, it is sensible to support the broadly held view that in despite of one's discontentment with Blair's failed foreign policy, it is a folly to destroy a great nation of Great Britain and its millions decent people – a nation that has given to many of us a shelter and decent schooling for our children.

Having said that, it is also obvious that Blair's loyalty to Bush and his unequivocal commitment to follow him to his war in Iraq without the United Nations' endorsement was another foolish and formidable mistake for a 21st-century British Prime Minister. Critiques from all world directions indicate that Bush and Blair 'BBs' have turned our world into unsafe place as a consequence of their ignorance or arrogance in tackling world terrorism. I completely agree with former Commander of SAS (Special Air Service) **General**

Sir Michael Rose, who sometimes ago called for Tony Blair be impeached and face trial over his illegal war in Iraq. The General was justified by stating that the Prime Minister should not be allowed to "walk away" from the fact that he took his country to war on false premise. The international Criminal Court of Justice in The Hague, Netherlands, was established not only for people in the weaker nations of the Third World, people like the late Slobodan Milosevic (Yugoslavia), Saddam Hussein (Iraq), Charles Taylor (Liberia) etc. To foster the genuineness of this international judiciary body, it is, I must call, to all fair-minded people who believe in justice for all, to support the line of pressure by the former General Rose to see Bush and Blair eventually facing justice for their reckless rush to an illegal war in Iraq.

In addition, in his February 2003 letter of resignation from US Foreign Service to the former US Secretary of State Colin Powell, **John Brady Kiesling**, political counselor of the US Embassy in Greece, was in my opinion, justified to emphasize the following:

> Our current course will bring instability and danger, not security. We should ask ourselves why we have failed to persuade more of the world that a war with Iraq is necessary.... We spread disproportionate terror and confusion in the public mind, arbitrarily linking the unrelated problems of terrorism and Iraq....

Many experts on terrorism have strongly warned that the US war on terrorism in Afghanistan and Iraq is non-winnable. The coalition forces led by the US have no enemy front lines to pound and cross; have no important enemy military and logistic bases to destroy; have no enemy air plane or fleets on waters to strike and so forth. The US (supported by the UK) is fighting powerless and very embarrassing Islamic fundamentalists in the dark rooms of the world – enemies who scare and have changed the way of life of the people in the most powerful nation on the Earth; Bush and Blair have dropped bombs which killed innocent Iraqi children in the vain hope to defeat the invisible Muslim extremist enemies; they both have convincingly endeavoured to pursue a long, costly and counter-productive war to stop radical Muslims who impose their ideology on the Western world by all means, including by violence and mass killings of innocent people, no matter if you are a Westerner or not; opponent to Islamic religion or not; religious believer or not, baby or not, and by even scarifying their own fellow Muslims, etc. The war between the West and Islam is a war of ideology – Western ideology versus Islamic ideology. Although one in the West may conclude that the winner of this ideological war will be the pacifist bestseller of its values across the world, however, it is worth to recall that Professor William Beeman, a specialist in Middle East culture at Brown University states this: "The root cause is not terrorist activity ... It is the relationship between the United States and the Islamic world. Until this central cancerous problem is treated, Americans [presumably Britons as their followers too] will never be free from fear."

Nevertheless, on Iraq's case, as it is stated earlier in the introduction, this country is simply referred in this book as an example of a good lesson to be learned on Tony Blair's foreign policy that sought to impose on weaker nations the will of the US and UK. It is obvious that Iraq is a relevant example to understanding why many people across the United Kingdom and the world, people like me, have declined their sympathy or detest the current US/UK foreign policy. Additionally, we need to be very careful in challenging the current US/UK bad foreign policy, and it has to be conveyed that Blair's abysmal handling of Iraq's crisis does not give anyone the right or red light to use any words that terrorise an entire British nation or bomb innocent people. Our dissatisfaction and anger over the US/UK foreign policy **MUST** be expressed through the submission and boundaries of British laws and conventional politics, which include common sense and constructive free expression. It is fair to conclude that no matter how much one's cause may attract the national and international public support, but sacrificing children by bombing them with a pretext of Bush and Blair's arrogance of power over other people and nations, is beyond any proportionate protest and an offence of high crime. Killing innocent people destroys one's good cause and gives the US/UK the chance to emerge as justified in imposing their will on other people behind Western values.

On Africa's aid, I am returning to Blair's Commission in Africa to accentuate (as it has been well-documented) that since 1981, the Irish musician Bob Geldof has been doing a remarkable charitable work in Africa. I deeply appreciate his generosity to Africans in need, particularly to African children in critical need. But I terribly lament that connecting his noble work (one for which he will be remembered forever) with Tony Blair, a man with a fresh blood of innocent Iraqis in his hands, is tantamount to connecting his decorous and gracious work and himself with an evil.

Further on Africa's aid, apart of the speech I have elaborated for him in the chapter one of this book, Blair has nothing left to tell Africans rather than playing game of promising them money from British taxpayers in order to divide the nations of the continent into groups of economically prosperous and non-prosperous. To make sense of this, his three consecutive addresses to the Labour party conference (2004, 2005 and 2006) have indicated something that suggest that Blair's premature forced departure from Number 10, means Blair's gradual shortage of speech. His pledging-speech on Africa in 2004 before May 2005 British general election was so passionate and longest in words – 114 words:

> Next year as president of the G8 along with action on climate change, we will try for consensus on a new plan for Africa, that not only on aid and trade but on conflict resolution, on fighting corruption, on the killer diseases Aids, malaria and TB, on education, water, infrastructure. A plan to lift that continent in hope and lift from ourselves the shame that so many human beings live and die in misery when we know together we could stop it; and when unchecked this misery some time, somewhere in the future will threaten us. But understand this reality. Little of it will happen except in alliance with the United States of America.

Blair's 2005 speech on Africa after winning the May general election was short in words – 62 words:

> And wasn't it an inspiration to hear the Prime Minister of Mozambique yesterday pay tribute to your Labour Government and think that only this Labour Government would have put Africa at the heart of the summit of the richest nations on earth; agreed action on HIV/AIDS and malaria, on debt relief and trade and got them to double aid, trebling it ourselves.

When people in the United Kingdom and Africa expected the departing British Prime Minister to tell them that he now knows about what went wrong on Africa's social and economic decline in the last past 25 years and emphasizes much more on the successes achieved by his established Commission on Africa, during his 2006 farewell speech to the Labour party conference in Manchester, Blair acknowledged himself that he had no more gimmicks to sell, and his speech on Africa on that occasion was the shortest one, limited to 32 word-long:

> Every day this Government has been in power, every day in Africa, children have lived who otherwise would have died because this country led the way in cancelling debt and global poverty.

Where Zimbabwe is concerned, Blair might not realised that his personal attitude to the person of President Mugabe would only be characterised by many people as an attitude of long-lasting rancor and neo-colonial attitude. For instance, his disdain attitude demonstrated during the Pope's funeral in Vatican, Italy, when he refused to sit closely alongside President Mugabe, has gone far beyond any uncivilised person. It might force many people to believe that Blair's contemptuous behaviour has been at the centre of the existing disquiet between Number 10 Downing Street and Harare since he came to power in 1997. This fact is reinforced by 'International Crisis Group' in its Executive Summary page xi of a book called 'Blood and Soil - 2004', where it highlights that: *"When a Labour government came to power in the UK in 1997, a sharp chill developed in British-Zimbabwean ties ....".*

I am now turning to some British politicians I wrote to in the course of last years to reveal some more cases related to British bad foreign policy. The following information reveals how British officials manifest their imperialist and neo-colonialist aggressive attitude towards other nations; how they manifest their long contemptuous behaviour for the principles of Sovereignty, non-interference and self-determination of nations and mutual cooperation between human beings:

1) Right Honourable Michael Ancram, (Conservative MP) is a co-founder member of the '2005 Henry Jackson Society', which the main objective is to sell the values of Western liberal democracy across the world, and if need be to impose it on other world nations through military intervention. In my opinion, there is no doubt that this military imposition to achieve its goals does not refer to the Giant nations such as Russia, China and even North Korea, but refers to world weaker nations. It is a laisser-faire that an organisation that holds a big danger for innocent people as we see in Iraq and presents negative consequences on British foreign policy, which has already lost its credibility in the world, has been allowed to operate in this country under British law, without people being interested or worrying. As it is known, many politicians at Westminster do not talk to dictators and terrorists, but Michael Ancram was the first British Minister to meet with Sinn Fein and the IRA (Irish Republican Army) for 25 years. More interestingly, not knowing how a war scene looks like, the British MP who supports British military action in order to impose the Western values of liberal democracy across the world, according to his biography, he had never been in the army before. Alongside his interest in politics and law, Michael Ancram has been much more involved in farming as a

partner in an arable tenanted farm in the Scottish Borders. His hobbies, alongside folk singing, include photography and skiing. However, while high ranking military officials who have been in war scenes are complaining about the present situation of our troops in Iraq, Ancram is prepared to send our children to war that interests his organisation, not one that interests British people. The kind of Michael Ancram in the British high political echelon means that in future Britain may end up provoking its own Armageddon.

Arriving at this point, it is safe to bring to light that with arrogant and aggressive British citizens in the British political apparatus, (citizens like Tony Blair, Michael Howard, Jack Straw, Michael Ancram and many other associates) Britain will become more and more a detested and fearful nation to many nations across the world. To stand any chance to reverse this trend and restore Britain's world credibility, damaged by distorted and bellicose foreign policy, in my viewpoint, there is a need for a popular demand to return people like Clare Short (Labour MP) to the high echelon of British politics and if need be to stand for British general election. Whatever her stance on the current domestic affairs of Zimbabwe and her discontentment towards Thabo Mbeki over Zimbabwe, however, Clare Short has been regarded by many fair-minded people as a decent and easy-to-read British politician – she is not viewed as the kind of those vicious politicians at Westminster who have no other option but, to inflame the political 'status quo' in Zimbabwe, influence division among its people with expectation to turn one group against another, culminating in national and regional turmoil and bloodshed. Clare is not among those brutal British politicians led by Blair, who scornfully are pursuing these imperialist and neo-colonialist goals, simultaneously, seeking support from countries in the Southern Africa region for a British invasion and "regime change" in Zimbabwe. Clare Short is also included in the group of good-natured British politicians who would not dare to commit British men and women in uniform to unpopular and counterproductive war, deliberately aimed at removing an abhorred world leader wherever in the world of weaker nations. While some Labour politicians at Number 10 are manipulated or blindly driven by Blair's personal political ambition or deliberately choose not challenge Blair's wrong political direction in handling international affairs in fear of loosing their prestigious and high ranking political positions, over Iraq row, Short has heroically given up her Cabinet position in the safeguard of her political conviction on the domestic and world affairs. I am satisfied with her political stance and her heroic example which deserves nothing more but a popular endorsement and praise. Well done Clare Short!

2) In respect to both British compassionate MPs Kate Hoey and Richard Benyon, questions abound: First, if the Labour Government has to authorise its MPs to use British taxpayers' money to travel across the world in spying missions, what is then the job of British journalists? Second, is that sensible that Richard Benyon should be too worried to take his justice first to Robert Mugabe for lack of democracy when justice is needed first for Tony Blair, a British Prime Minister who lied to his people and took Britain to an illegal and unpopular war in Iraq? Are British soldiers supposed to sacrifice their lives for a war based on Blair's false premise to achieve his own personal political goals on the world stage?

3: With reference to Westminster's stance on Zimbabwe, through my correspondence with Miss Ana McIntosh (Conservative MP) and many other British MPs/politicians referred in this book, I found that many of them may be relying on the general and old British foreign policy information on Zimbabwe and Africa as a whole. I deeply appreciate the time and interest taken by McIntosh in replying to my letters, but I am afraid that her letters to me reveal that she might lack her own understanding and findings on updated African reality and facts. It is very simple to notice this unpalatable fact if we compare the contents in her five-page letter (in the appendix 4) addressed to me and the contents in another letter (also in appendix 4) from Andrew Hopkinson at Foreign and Commonwealth Office – Southern Africa Department.

Furthermore, in the context of this book, it was hardly and positively written out based of my personal knowledge on British foreign policy towards Africa and Africa's reality. It is a book written to benefit the majority of Zimbabwean people, and African people as a whole. However, although I would expect people to support this demanding initiative to expose and challenge British up-side reality of Africa, it is also obvious to expect that handful of people would ask how can someone who is neither Zimbabwean nor had never been in Zimbabwe understand what has been going on there. Others would interpret this book as supportive of African leaders, particularly supportive of Thabo Mbeki and Robert Mugabe. To these people, it is imperative to anticipate that I am prepared to learn from people what I do not know about Africa rather than wasting time to listening to impertinent questions and non-constructive comments by those desperate Africans who have been selling themselves in the European cities in hope to be placed in power in

African countries by their former colonial masters. Further to this, it would be an interesting opportunity to recall to them that when Angola (my original country) assisted Zimbabwean people to liberate from the appalling human existence under the white minority regime led by the African white fascist Ian Smith, no Zimbabwean or anyone else tempted to ask why Angolans did so if they were not Zimbabweans.

When Angola, gained its independence from Portugal through a bitter-ness armed anti-colonial struggle in 1975, it had extended its struggle to all Africa to contribute in the liberation of all African countries which had still been under colonialism and apartheid. This struggle was even extended further to elsewhere outside Africa, in the concrete case, to East Timor in far Asia. By any reasonable standard of judgement, Angola could not be a safe and stable country in the region where other countries were still under colonial occupation and apartheid system. Angolan authorities knowing too well the entailed price of helping other countries in the region to liberate from those European evil political systems, nevertheless, they devised many ant-imperial-ist and anti-colonial slogans which, if my memory is still accurate, included: *"A continuação da nossa luta está na Africa do Sul, Namibia, Zimbabwe, Sahara do Oest, Palestina e Timor do Lest."* (*The continuation of our struggle is in South Africa, Namibia, Zimbabwe, Western Sahara, Palestine and East Timor*). As a result, Angolan people had massively paid in blood and deaths from regular military attacks by the then South Africa apartheid. Angola suffered apartheid military attacks of all types that were aimed at preventing Namibia's SWAPO (South West African People's Organisation) and South African ANC (African National Congress) from liberating their people from dehumanising colonial-ism and hidebound apartheid system ever known in any part of this world, except in Southern Africa region. As a neighbouring country to Zimbabwe and South Africa, the then newly independent Mozambique had also paid the same price as a result of helping Zimbabwean and South African people to liberate from both fascists/evils Ian Smith and Peter W. Botha.

As a genuine African citizen, to understand the sacrifice of people who are historically bound to common struggle against colonialism and neo-co-lonialism, and people who have a moral responsibility to each other, it is worth to give it a moment's thought the mystery that surrounded the Sunday night 19/10/1986 Tupolev 134A jetliner crash that killed Samora Machel, African revolutionary and first President of Mozambique. The President's plane was travelling from Lusaka, capital city of Zambia, over Zimbabwe and Mozambique to Maputo when it crashed within South African territory. It went down to a side of hill belonging to the Lebombo's mountains in the Mbuzini area, the corner of the eastern Transvaal, near the junction of the Mozambican, Swazi and South African borders. Although there had never been a formal accusation on the accident by any Mozambican officials, the second and former President of Mozambique, Joaquim Chissano, once said in June 1987 that "President Samora's death was no accident." Samora Machael's death might have been the price that Mozambique had paid as a consequence of its commitment to the complete eradication of colonialism, neo-colonialism and apartheid in Africa. Samora's death concerns Africans and that is why to the present date, questions from all Africa's directions on unsolved causes of his plane crash still abound.

When in the earlier 1980's the Angolan Government sent me to Cuba for further military preparation, it did so for me to defend not only the people of Angola but all people of African continent (including people of Zimbabwe) from imperialist and neo-colonial domination and Western interference in affairs of African subjugated nations. Zimbabwe matters for fair-minded Africans, and if they allow an aggressive and reckless Tony Blair to turn this great nation of Africa into a failed state, the disastrous consequences will be felt not only in Zimbabwe, but beyond its borders, as we are witnessing in Iraq. Thabo Mbeki is therefore justified to step in and prevent Blair's imperialist invasion of his neighbour that will only bring the bulk of trouble of a failed Zimbabwe on the South Africa's shoulders. It is also safe to point out that any popular resentment or revolutionary struggle against British neo-colonial ambitions in Zimbabwe, will in fact, attract unconditional support and engage all regional countries within the SADC (Southern Africa Development Community). – At least, let us not be ignorant of this fact.

Finally, I have no snobbish disdain for anyone who wants to engage in constructive debate and criticism. I am not worried at all about many British politicians who will found the contents in this book not comforting their imperialist objectives, but for those Africans, who have been the forefronts of their former colonialist masters in Africa, my response to them will remain as following:

First of all, nobody has the right to stop me from criticising any British misrepresentation or misperception of African people and their crucial problems;

• I have the right to oppose any imperialist language employed by British politicians which negatively characterise African leaders;

• I do not need to go first to Zimbabwe to research and understand what was stipulated in the '1979 Lancaster House Agreement' which led the people of Zimbabwe to independence in 1980;

• I do not need to be a Zimbabwean citizen to know that President Robert Mugabe had served 10 years in prison under Rhodesian white minority rule led by the atrocious white African Ian Smith;

• I do not need to be in Zimbabwe to properly listen and understand President Thabo Mbeki's position on land issue in Zimbabwe and his quite diplomacy, which is not appreciated at Westminster;

• I do not need to go to Zimbabwe to learn that President Mugabe has been regarded as one the greatest leaders in the African history, and how much support he enjoys in the Southern region of Africa, African Union, United Nations and other international organisations;

• Many people in Britain did not need to go first to Rhodesia and South Africa before engaging themselves in protest against Ian Smith's illegal regime and apartheid system;

• Some British politicians who are currently debating and criticising African governments' performance in the House of Commons had never put their feet in Africa before. I was born and grew up in Africa and worked for the Angolan Government some years ago;

• For whatever reasons, any genuine Zimbabwean or African cannot take for granted or tolerate the disrespectful and insulting comments made by British MP Michael Ancram on British national TV, when he stated: *"when we left [Zimbabwe] there was enough food..." – "Zimbabwe was, for many years, the breadbasket of Africa producing enough food not simply to feed itself but to feed much of the continent.."*. Therefore, do I need permission from someone before I ask Ancram, who were the backbone producers of the breadbasket that he refers to? Or does he intend to return to Zimbabwe's fertile land to continue to exploit poor Zimbabwean/African workers to produce that breadbasket for British economic profits?

• Do I need permission from Zimbabweans before I ask Tony Blair, Michael Ancram, Kate Hoey, Richard Benyon, etc, who are invited Britain to change regime in Zimbabwe, and who will be the most beneficiaries of that change? Etc.

Appendix 1

The bitterness and long-lasting land question in Zimbabwe:

a) Pre-Independence legislation on land

b) Post-Independence legislation on land

Appendix 1

In discussing the current situation in Zimbabwe, which the land is at the centre of the crisis, it would be unwise for anyone just to assume that President Robert Mugabe woke up one morning and told war veterans and other demonstrators to seize white farms, as sometimes it has been suggested by the Western politicians and press. Instead, it would be wise first to recognise, if not by looking at the land question in Africa as a whole, in Zimbabwe, among other important issues, the land has indeed remained the most crucial political and economic issue of that southern African country. Whereas, anyone who wants to understand what is happening in Zimbabwe and form a real picture on the importance of land issue in Africa, will need enough patience to look at the facts and events in the history of Zimbabwe. To help many readers who for any reason have not had the opportunity or access to the crucial documents on land question in Zimbabwe, I propose, for their further knowledge to insert in the following pages some information which have been extracted from some official documents made available to me by the Zimbabwe high Commission in United Kingdom, based in London. It will include the Zimbabwe pre-Independence and post-Independence legislation on land:

THE BITTERNESS AND LONG-LASTING LAND QUESTION IN ZIMBABWE:

A. LAND ISSUE – FACT SHEET

1.0. PRE-INDEPENDENCE LEGISLATION ON LAND:

Throughout the history of Zimbabwe, land has remained the most important political and economic issue in the country. This can be traced back to the time of the pioneer Column in the late 1800s and the subsequent legal instruments that were passed and entrenched to ensure division of the ownership of land between the two major races namely, blacks and whites. The evolution of these legal instruments is as follows.

1.1. The Lippert Concession (1889):

This Concession which preceded the actual occupation of Zimbabwe in 1890 allowed would-be settlers to acquire land rights from the indigenous people. The act resulted in the British South African Company (BSAC) buying concessions from the British Monarch which were then used as the basis of land expropriation. The revenue accrued was repatriated to the United Kingdom and the indigenous peoples, the owners of the land, got nothing.

1.2. The Native Reserves Order in Council (1898)

The order created the infamous Natives Reserves for blacks only. This was in the face of a systematic mass land expropriation by white settlers. To the whites, the Native reserves were meant to prevent the extinction of the indigenous people while at the same time guaranteeing that settlers got the lion's share of fertile land. The result was that Native Reserves were set up haphazardly in low potential areas which subsequently became the present Communal areas.

1.2. 1890-1920 Period

This was a period of conquest and land expropriation.
The BSAC was in the forefront of the occupation of Mashonaland and Matebeleland and the suppression of the first Chimurenga (National Uprising in 1893). These processes we re accompanied by the seizure of land and cattle. Racial segregation in the use and ownership of land was introduced at an earlier stage. By the eve of World War One in 1914, the apportionament of land was as follows:
Africans 24 000 000 acres
The BSAC 48 000 000 acres
Individual white settlers 13 000 000 acres
Other Private Companies 9 000 000 acres
During this period, the country's population was as follows:

African population 836 000
Whites 28 000

Even by this earlier period, only 3% of the population controlled 75% of the economically productive land while 97%
were forcefully confined to 23% of the land scattred into a
number of reserves.

1.3. The Land Apportionment Act (1930)
The main purpose of the act was to formalise separation by
law, law between blacks and whites, and this was after the
deliberation and recommendations of the Morris Carter
Commission of 1925. The fertile high rainfall areas became
large scale privately owned white farms. In 1931, the act
divided the land area in the country as follows:
Land classification acreage
Native Reserves 29 000 000 acres
Native Purchase Areas 8 000 000 acres
European areas 49 000 000 acres
Unassigned 6 000 000 acres
Forest 3 000 000 acres
Population distribution was as follows:
Africans: 1.1 million
Whites: 50 000

1.5. Native Land Husbandry Act (1951):
The Act meant to enforce private ownership of land, destock-
ing and conservation practices on black small holders. It met
mass resistance and fuelled nationalistic politics. The law was
subsequently scrapped in 1961.

1.6. The Tribal Trust Lands (TTL) Act (1965):
The Act was devised to change the name of the Native
Reserves and create trustees for the land. High population
densities on TTLs made them degraded 'homelands'.

2.0. Lancaster House Conference: The Land Debate.

2.1 In the Opening Speech to the Lancaster House Constitution,
the Patriotic Front listed the land question among its nine
major issues for negotiation. During the negotiation, the
British government insisted on a stringent protection of pri-

vate property with equally strict provisions for 'prompt' and 'adequate' compensation in the few cases where compulsory was to be allowed. The patriotic Front's position was that: every person was to be protected from having his property compulsorily acquired, subject to the right of government so acquired would be at the discretion of the government.

2.2. The patriotic Front objected to the British proposals as the objective of the struggle in Zimbabwe was the recovery of the land which the people were dispossessed of. The British provisions converted the freedom from deprivation of property into a right to retain privileges and perpetuate social and economic injustice.

2.3 The Lancaster House Conference nearly broke-down over the land question. The Patriotic Front wanted the British government to provide money to pay compensation. An agreement was reached and the Patriotic Front announced it as follows:

"We have now obtained assurances that... Britain, the United States of America and other countries will participate in a multinational donor effort to assist in land, agricultural and economic development programmes. These assurances go a long way in allaying the great concern we have over the whole land question arising from the great need our people have for land and our commitment to satisfy that need when in government".

2.4. At independence in 1980, 97% of our population (Africans) owned only 45 million acres, slightly under half the total area of 96 million acres, leaving the rest, over half the land area to only 3% of the population (whites). Such imbalances had to be redressed within the confines of the Lancaster House Constitution. Britain pledged to fund the resettlement programme to make sure that provisions for compulsory acquisition without compensation did not go into the Zimbabwean Constitution generally, and in particular through Section 16 which was designed to give total protection to private property.

2.5. Due to variety of reasons, all of which have their roots in the Lancaster House Agreement, the resettlement programme did not perform to expectations. Firstly, under the will-

148

ing/willing buyer principle, land was not offered in sufficient bulk to the government. Secondly, that which was offered to government was the poorer qualify land in regions of low rainfall patterns and poor ecological soils. Thirdly, because of the 'fair market price' clause, the government was greatly constrained and there have not been sufficient funds forthcoming to buy the land.

2.6.   In 1980 the Zimbabwe Conference on Reconstruction and Development (ZIMCORD) conference was held and its stated objective of mobilising support from the international community was for, *inter alia,* finance for resettlement. Participants in the scheme were Britain, West Germany, the United States of America and others. The aid promised at Lancaster and ZIMCORD was not forthcoming in sufficient amounts of extinguish land hunger. Thus after seven years of independence only 40 000 families of the original 162 000 families were settled between 1980 and 1987.

3.0.   POST INDEPENDENCE LEGISLATION ON LAND:
The nationalist movement and the cry for freedom was, among other things, born of the need to change the skewed land distribution pattern in the country. Even during the Lancaster House talks in London in 1979, the land issue was so cardinal to the independence of Zimbabwe that it was enshrined in the constitution of independent Zimbabwe. The negotiating parties agreed that there would be no compulsory acquisition of land but that a willing seller/willing buyer principle would apply for the first ten years.

3.1.   <u>The Communal Land (1981)</u>
The Act was designed to change TTLs into Communal Areas which resulted in the shift of land authority from traditional leadership to local authorities.

3.2.   <u>The Land Acquisition Act (1985)</u>
The Act drawn up in the spirit of the Lancaster House Agreement of 1979, (willing seller/willing buyer principle) gave government the first right to purchase large scale farms for resettlement of indigenous people. Largely because of financial constraints, the act had a limited impact on the resettlement programme.

4.0. Land Reform and Resettlement Programme
The desire to resettle the landless by the government has not been
fulfilled largely because the government could not acquire land
when and where it desire. Land owners were either unwilling to
sell or asked for double or triple the prices for their land. Because
of the willing seller/willing buyer undertaking, government could
only settle 71 000 families out of a targeted 162 families between
1980 and 1990.

Meanwhile, the level of congestion reached catastrophic levels.
Political pressure for redress mounted, and in some instances,
communal farmers settled themselves unilaterally and haphazardly on commercial farms bordering their areas.

Against this background, the government decided to compulsorily acquire land for resettlement using the Land Acquisition Act
(Chapter 2010). The act provides for fair compensation for land
acquired for resettlement purposes. The landowner has recourse to
court if not agreeable to the price set by the acquiring authority.

4.1. The Land Acquisition Act (1992)
This act is a follow-up to the 1985 Act and is meant to
acquire more land for the resettlement of blacks that are in
congested marginal rainfall areas. Implementation of this act
is currently underway.

4.1.1. Criteria for Land Acquisition
The land targeted for acquisition was categorised as fol-
lows:
• Derelict land
• Under-utilised land
• Land owned by absentee-landlords
• Land from farmers with more than one farm or with
oversized farms (defined according to what is sustain-
able under given ecological Conditions)
• Land adjacent to communal areas.

Those who feel that their land should not have been designated are asked to submit (to government) their written
objections (as per the requirements of the act) within 30 days
of the notice to compulsorily acquire being gazetted.

4.2.   Donors Conference and the Second Phase of the Land
       Reform and Resettlement (LRRP): September 1998.
       The international Donors' Conference on Land Reform and
       Resettlement Programme in Zimbabwe was held in Harare
       from 9-11 September, 1998. The objective of the Conference
       was to inform the donor community on the land reform and
       resettlement programme and to mobilise support for the
       same, About 48 countries and international organisations
       were represented at the Conference.

       The donors unanimously endorsed the need for the land
       reform and resettlement in Zimbabwe and affirmed that the
       programme was essential for poverty reduction, economic
       growth and stability. They also appreciated the political im-
       perative and urgency of the Land Reform and Resettlement
       Programme and agreed that the Inception Phase covering 24
       months should start immediately.

       A number of donors pledged technical and financial support
       for the programme.

4.3.   Objectives of the Land and Resettlement Programme:
       To reduce the extent and intensity of poverty among rural
       families and farm workers by providing them adequate land
       for agricultural use. Communal families have contributed a
       lot to agricultural produce.

       To increase the contribution of agriculture to GDP by
       increasing the number of commercialised small-scale farmers
       using formerly under utilised

       To promote the environmentally sustainable utilisation of
       land

       To increase the conditions for sustainable peace and social
       stability by removing imbalances in land ownership

4.4.   Beneficiaries of the Resettlement Programme:
       Communal families selected from overpopulated villages,
       including ex-farm workers and ex-mine workers.

       People with training or certificates in agriculture or a dem-
       onstrated capacity in farming such as Master Farmers and

graduates from agricultural colleges.

Special groups such as women who constitute 51% of the population

Indigenous people intent on making a break-through in commercial agriculture.

5.0.   The Government and Resettlement Models:
The following are the proposed resettlement models to be implemented:

5.1.   MODEL A1 (Villagised)
Each settler is allocated a residential plot and an individual arable plot, with communally shared grazing wood-lots and water points.

5.2.   MODEL A2 (Self-Constrained Units)
Each settler is given a self-contained complete unit with residential, arable and grazing lot.

5.3.   THREE TIER MODEL

This model is applicable to the drier parts of the country where Ranching is the only sustainable land use. The land is divided into three tiers as follows:

First Tier: Comprising a cluster of villages, with some arable plots and space for social services.

Second Tier: Each benefiting household keeps a limited number of Livestock units for day to day use.

Third Tier: This is the main grazing area where the bulk of the herd is kept for commercial purposes.

6.0.   Alter Land Acquisition and Resettlement Approaches.

6.1.   Community participation and implementation model
In this model the government acquires the land, and communities plan and execute their own settlement. They are also responsible for obtaining the required planning, technical, and managerial assistance from any source they choose, including government services, NGOs, or the private sector.

Once the government has acquired the land and has selected and trained the beneficiaries, it disburses the remaining balance of the Uniform public support to the beneficiary community and lets it plan and execute its own settlement. The balance could be disbursed in tranches, which could be subject to demonstration of progress in planning (to be kept very simple) and execution of the development.

6.2. <u>Private sector approaches</u>

Public support for privet sector-initiated approaches would have the advantage of widening the scope and increasing the efficiency of the land reform programme by enhancing the commercialisation of smallholder agriculture, providing land reform beneficiaries with access to the private sector partner's business infrastructure, knowledge and information, and encouraging private sector contribution to the programme.

The potential implementing agencies for the private sector approaches could be: farmers' associations (or their individual members as sellers or developers), commercial banks (or group of banks), private sector developers, labours unions, churches, women's organisations, and other NGOs. As described above, a potential implementing organisation would first need to have its specific programme proposal screened and be accredited by the co-ordinating entity. The scheme could involve an entire farm or any subdivision thereof.

The total costs (land transactions and development costs) would be financed by the uniform public support and a loan from a private bank, as well as by own equity contributions in cash, kind or labour, and any other private contributions the seller or the beneficiaries may be able to mobilise.

Once the settlement project is developed, it is presented to the bank for financing, either in the form of a group loan, individual loan, or a combination of the two. The disbursement of the public support to the seller of the land, agents, developers or beneficiaries could be handled by the same bank which provides the loan.

The actual loan terms would be defined by the financial intermediary (bank). The interest rate would be the going market rate for long-term real estate loans as defined by the financial intermediary. A grace period could be granted, two or three years perhaps, and the full term could be around ten or fifteen years.

The private sector approach can have many variations:

6.2.1 individual homesteads with garden

6.2.2 communities who hold land as a condominium or under communal tenure;

6.2.3 contract farming with the former owner or another commercial farmer or estate;

6.2.4 an irrigated model with market gardening for communities made up of female headed households; families willing to adopt up orphans or squatters; and

6.2.5 Equity participation schemes with the former or a new owner of a commercial farm.

6.3. Community land purchase model

This model has many similarities to model 1 and 2, but it differs from them in that the community is in the driver seat for all decisions, while the implementing organisation only has enabling, supervisory, and disbursement functions. Most importantly, communities not only plan and execute their own settlement, but also search for the land they want to purchase and negotiate the price with the seller. Implementing agencies for this model may be local governments, the Community Action Fund, or a private entity such as a bank or a consortium of banks.

In all other respects the community land purchase model is executed like a combination of the community participation and execution model, and the private sector models. All variants of the latter could be considered as options by the land purchasing community.

7.0 The government of Zimbabwe estimates that the total cost of the land reform and resettlement programme is USS1.1 billion. This will cover costs of;

154

Land acquisition and development.
Infrastructure and services (roads, water, first crop tillage schools and clinics).
Farmer support and credit facilities.

B. CONCLUSION
THE LAND QUESTION: NOT JUST POLITICS OR AN ELECTION ISSUE

The demonstrations on farms by war veterans and the government's efforts to resolve the land question once and for all are not just about elections or politics as has been erroneously suggested by some press groups in the West.

They are manifestations of a long-standing struggle by the indigenous people to claim what is rightfully theirs. They are part of sustained and justified efforts over the last century to reverse historical injustices that had been perpetrated by successive colonial regimes through systematic dispossession of indigenous people under various legislative provisions backed by coercive state machinery.

History is replete with incidences of resistance by the indigenous people against forcible eviction from their ancestral lands. In the 60s Chief Rekai Tangwena and his Gairezi people fought a heroic but losing battle against the might of the colonial government to resist movement from their lands. Not even the law courts would assist the Gairezi people. Their principled stand was however an inspiration to the liberation struggle which was mainly about land. The Lancaster House Constitution which ushered in Zimbabwe's independence, unfortunately did not adequately address the issue of land redistribution. Indeed, the Lancaster House negotiations almost broke down on the issue of land and only proceeded after the British and American Government gave assurances that funds would be provided for the resettlement programme.

Restrictive clauses in the Lancaster House Constitution together with conditions attached to British funding such as the "willing buyer - willing seller" clauses severely hampered the pace of the resettlement programme. After the amendment of the Lancaster House Constitution and the promulgation of the Land Acquisition Act of 1992 the programme continued to be hampered bi inadequate funding since the British had unilaterally abrogated their commitment to provide funds. Furthermore some farmers delayed the process by tying up intended land acquisition in the law courts.

The Government convened the 1998 Land Donor Conference hoping to come up with a conclusive and long lasting resolution acceptable to all the stakeholders. Regrettably, none of the pledges made at the Donor Conference have been honoured, and for a purpose. Commenting on the withholding by Britain of money pledged at the Conference, the Business Day (South Africa) on 27 May 2000 stated this: "This was part of a scheme to drive Mugabe and his ZANU (PF) party out of office. The idea was to force Mugabe to hold elections without letting him fulfil his promises on land, thus undermining his popular support".

The people of Zimbabwe have therefore had to endure along and frustrating wait for the return of their lands. Contrary the most Western Press reports, the demonstrations on land are not a new phenomenon. In 1998, the svosve people evidently frustrated by the long wait initiated land occupations as a desperate measure to regain their birthright. At the time the government was able to persuade them to await the outcome of the Land Donor Conference. It is now a matter of history that no resources have been availed to Zimbabwe to speed up the resettlement programme. The land acquisition clause in the Draft Constitution therefore provided for many an opportunity for a breakthrough in the long standing issue. When it was rejected, it equally dashed their hopes and brought their frustrations to the fore. The war veterans who had sacrified so much including staking their lives to regain land thus led the current demonstrations. It is therefore a gross misrepresentation to say that the land issue is being used to divert attention from economic problems such as employment. The provision of land to the landless will in actual fact contribute to reducing unemployment and alleviation of poverty by empowering the significant number of Zimbabwean citizens to engage in productive self-employment. Zimbabweans citizens have always demonstrated their close affinity to the land and their capacity to be agriculturally productive. The argument that agricultural production will decline flies in the face of the reality that the indigenous Zimbabweans are the backbone of agricultural production even on the white owned commercial farms.

There have been unfounded allegations that land that has been acquired for resettlement before has been given to government cronies and partly faithful. The allegation ignores the fact that the Land Reform programme has a number of schemes designed to suit the requirements of different categories of applicants. Indeed those among the indigenous population who have the resources to engage in commercial farming purposes. This scheme is open to all Zimbabweans and has been in existence since colonial times, but at the time was only reserved as a privilege for the white members of the community.

The Government has avoided the path of confrontation against the war veterans and other demonstrators currently occupying some farms. The police have explained in their representations to the Courts that they do not have resources to forcibly evict the demonstrators and are in any case of the view that such an action would most likely result in greater bloodshed and public disorder. The demonstrations have remained largely peaceful save for a few regrettable incidences, which have resulted in loss of life. The Government has since amended the Constitution and put in place enabling legislation for the conclusive resolution of the land question. It will remain guided by clear principles in targeting land for acquisition. In this regard, only under-utilized land, land owned by absentee landlords and land from farmers who own multiple farms will be acquired. No owner with only one farm will be dispossessed. If a farm is in an area that has been designated for resettlement, a replacement farm will be provided. The Government will pay for improvements to the owners of farms acquired for resettlement. It is imperative for the Government to resolve the land question once and for all for long term economic, social and moral justice.

Appendix 2

Response to allegations of deaths suffered during operation murambatsvina/ restore order by Zimbabwean Government in summer 2005

Appendix 2

RESPONSE TO ALLEGATIONS OF DEATHS SUFFERED DURING OPERATION MURAMBATSVINA/RESTORE ORDER

INTRODUCTION

This document is prompted by paragraph 6.5.1 **"Right to Life and Property"** in the UN Special Envoy Mrs A. K. **TIBAUUKA** report.

From the onset, it is important and factual to state that no death was occasioned by Operation Murambatsvina/Restore Order at Porta Farm during the clean up exercise. This report covers six deaths which occurred but not caused by the operation as reported. The true circumstances are given below.

CASE 1

On 19 June 2005 and at 1400 hours, deceased Robert **MUTUSVA** who was in the company of his brother Tapiwa **MUTUSVA** and a friend TSIKA joined in pulling down the illegal structure at Number 4231 Unit D Seke Chitungwiza. While they were busy destroying the structure, a wall with a height of 1.2 metres and a diameter of 9 inches collapsed over the deceased hitting him on the head and left leg.

Chipo **CHIPANDA** N.R. 49-040661 AM9 of the same address, who was sitting in the main house heard a big bang and went out to investigate.

Tapiwa told her that a wall had fallen on the deceased. He was subsequently rushed to Chitungwiza hospital in an arrrbulance and was later referred to Harare Hospital where he died at 1900 hours.

At the time of the incident the Police were not at the scene. The Police had not yet entered into Unit D Seke, Chitungwiza since they were still in St Mary's area. A friend and brothers of tMe deceased were destroying the structure, as they knew it was illegal.

Police Zengeza Report Received Book (RRB) reference number 0766740
refers.

CASE 2

On 19 June 2005 and at 1330 hours, Alien **DANGA** N.R. 59-0677744-T-85 aged 20 years of Number 8667 Unit K Seke, Chitungwiza and Tinashe
MAPFUMO N.R. 59-086695-S-26 aged 19 years of Number 8668 Unit K Seke, Chitungwiza were demolishing an illegal structure at their residence.

While the two were busy destroying the structure it happened that the infant Terrence MUNYAKA aged one and half years of 8695 Unit K, Seke Chitungwiza was behind the same structure, which was being destroyed.

The structure fell and hit the infant. The two were not aware of the presence of the infant.

The infant sustained head injuries and was rushed to Chitungwiza Hospital were upon arrival, he was pronounced dead. Deceased's Father is Mutombo **MUNYAKA** a member of the Force stationed at Support Unit Headquarters.

At the time of the incident the Police task team had not reached the area.

The Police were still in St Mary's area and had not yet reached Seke area.

Police attended the scene and the body was taken for Post Mortem.

Chitungwiza RRB reference number 0881877 refers.

CASE 3

On 8 June 2005 and at 1040 hours, the deceased's parents Levada **RICHARD** (Mother) and Herbert **NYIKA** (Father) were destroying their two-roomed cabin at House Number 3446 Old Tafara, Mabvuku. During the process of destroying the cabin, their child Charmaine NYIKA was at a distance from the wall. There wasn't any close attention given to her.

The child started walking towards the mother, and when she was about to pass the wall, it fell over her and was trapped under the bricks. She was retrieved alive and was rushed to Mabvuku polyclinic where she was pronounced dead on arrival. Mabvuku C. R. 100/06/05. The Police were not at the scene when the demolitions were occurring.

CASE 4

On 21 June 2005 and at 0900 hours the now deceased Farai **BANWA** N.R. 59-096363 B 59 aged 18 of Number 11364 Zengeza 4 Chitungwiza was demolishing illegal structure when a lintel fell on him. He died instantly.

Informant Petronella ZIMUTO aged 25 who is a lodger at the same address witnessed the incident and later went to make a report at Zengeza Police Station, body of the deceased was taken to Chitungwiza Hospital Mortuary for Post Mortem.

Deceased was demolishing his illegal structure in compliance with the on going Operation Clean Up code-named "Murambatsvina". No police team on operation was near the place when the incident occurred Zengeza RRB 0766748 refers.

CASE 5

Sergeant **DAHWE** who was a member of the Zimbabwe Republic Police died on June 4, 2005 as a result of injuries sustained when they were destroying an illegal structure in Old Magwegwe, Bulawayo on June 29, 2005. Sergeant **DEHWE** was part of a group of officers and civilians destroying in the suburb and in the process a wall fell on him and a civilian member identified as Sylvester SIBANDA. SIBANDA sustained a broken leg.

CASE 6

False Report

An SW Radio report to the effect that four people had died as a direct result of Operation **Murambatsvina** is false. An investigation carried out at Porta Farm has revealed that there was only one child who was killed in a road accident which was not in any way related to the Operation neither was a Zimbabwe Republic Police or Zimbabwe National Army vehicle involved.

The circumstances of the accident are that:
> It occurred on June 29, 2005 at about 1400 hours at the 29.5 km pegmark along the Harare-Bulawayo road.
> The vehicle involved is a Mitsubishi lorry registration number 854-679L owned by Greatermans (Pvt) Ltd. At the time of the accident it was being driven by Busuman **KATEVA** of 4331 Tongogara Street, Dzivarasekwa.
> The accident occurred at the 29.5 km peg when the deceased Fanandi **MANYERE** (4) and her mother both of 113 Porta Farm attempted to cross the road in front of the oncoming lorry. The mother managed to cross but the lorry hit the daughter who had been left behind. The daughter died on the spot

Norton Police attended and the accident is being investigated under

Norton reference TAB 181/05. The accident spot is a known accident black spot because of the Porta farm settlement along the busy Highway.

CONCLUSION

All Police operations are properly planned and executed with due regard to human rights issues, gender issues and the rights of children. Sufficient warnings are always given before the Police finally interface with the public; hence people demolished illegal structures on their own after notification and before arrival of the Police. In Operation Restore Order, Police had been approached by local authorities to help in enforcing Council by-laws which were being ignored. Police were, also specifically asked by the Local Authorities to assist City Councils to relocate street kids, vagrants, touts and vendors who were causing chaos in town. Police complied and assisted.

(REFERENCE: RESPONSE BY GOVERNMENT OF ZIMBABWE TO THE REPORT BY THE UN SPECIAL ENVOY ON OPERATION MURAMBATSVINA/RESTORE ORDER PUBLISHED IN JULY 2005)

Appendix 3

Quoted public opinions on why Zimbabwe matters and opinions on the contentious relations between Zimbabwe and Britain.

Appendix 3

IS MUGABE A HERO TO AFRICANS?

Given the fact that many British MPs/politicians and media have been reticent to recognise at least the good side of many African leaders; and also given the fact that many British people have their minds implanted with false perception that Robert Mugabe is nothing else but an evil fascist African Leader, who has done nothing virtuous for Zimbabwe and Africa, to reverse this British neo-colonialist propaganda, I thought it proper to include in this appendix some relevant quoted public opinions from http://news.bbc.co.uk/1/hi/world/africa/3292151.stm12/01/2004 – BBCNEWS World Africa Does Zimbabwe matter to Africa?

1. "What concerns and troubles most Africans and most fair-minded people around the world are the blatant double standards in this matter by Britain and Australia. These are the same countries that want Pakistan re-admitted to the Commonwealth for "helping with the war on terrorism" (something that the West perceives to be closest to its interests) while at the same time campaigning for the continued suspension of Zimbabwe. The real reason for Zimbabwe's exclusion is the balatant [blatant] racial politics of supporting a tiny minority's domination of the economy of Zimbabwe, not the otherwise understandable reason of sanctioning that country's government for stealing an election. If stealing elections leads to suspension from the Commonwealth, why has Nigeria not been expelled yet? The difference is of course that in Nigeria's case, no British or Australian interests are at stake. This is an absolute scandal."

Dr. Obiora Okafor – Nigeria

2. "Yes, Zimbabwe matters to Africa just like any other African country. In any case, quitting from Commonwealth is a blessing. I wish to call upon all African states to quit the Commonwealth because that will redeem their pride and independence. The Commonwealth only reminds me of those dark days when the 'great' Britain conquered our beloved countries. I don't think we should continue being Britain's colonies. Remember those days of slavery, hut tax, land grabbing, mineral exploitation etc? I salute Zimbabwe for its decision. VIVA AFRICA!"

Bosch – Botswana

3. "The importance of Zimbabwe to Africa cannot certainly be questionned, [questioned] especially at this time when international institutions such as the Commonwealth are putting in every effort to sever the brotherhood that is characteristic of Africa. In fact, Zimbabwe's indefinite suspension is the biggest blunder that the Commonwealth has had to commit in history, as it further confirms that the plight of Africa has hardly ever been the concern of the Commonwealth. Zimbabwe's problems have been created by the British who believe, they have the right to control the destiny of all other peoples. If we equate Zimbabwe's situation to HIV/AIDS, only then can we understand that stigma, isolation and discrimination is no solution to HIV/AIDS. It is time African states defend their pride by dissociating themselves from these colonial continuities. Mugabe is a hero. Who in the Commonwealth has a better human rights record? And whose human right?"

Divine F. Fuh – Botswana

4. "How does Australia treat asylum seekers and native **Balcks**? How does New Zealand treat its native Blacks? Mugabe is actually the only Black voice in the world fighting for the black woman and the black man dignity. The third Chimurenga must be won. I wish other Commonwealth black leaders will be courageous enough to suspend Britain, Australia and New Zealand (from the Commonwealth). Long live Zimbabwe! Long live Mugabe! Long life Zanu-PF! Down with the neocolonialistic MDC! Long live the Black Liberation! UHURU!"

Shungu M. Tundanonga-Dikunda – DR Congo/Germany

5. "Zimbabwe matters not only to Africa but to the world! That is why Britian [Britain] fuses over Zimbabwe, because they know they cannot get what they want, Zimbabwe's rich mineral resources. Which African nation does not harass its media or intimidate the opposition or violate human rights?"

Sarah Kinyoda – UK

6. "Zimbabwe matters a lot to the Africans and it is time they stand up against the British-inspired assault on Africa in general and Zimbabwe in particular. Britain, led by Tony Blair, is not after the interest of Zimbabweans

as a whole. It is after the interest of white minority who own the majority of the arable land in Zimbabwe."

Mohamed Yabarag – London, UK

7. "What kind of question is this? "Should Zimbabwean politics concern the rest of Africa?" Is there more to this question than meets the eye? Zimbabwe matters to Africa, but no more than any other African Country matters. Are you trying to suggest that it should matter in a rather different way? Zimbabwe has been made to appear more important to Africa than it really is. You Westerners are very funny! But we aren't as dumb as you think we are!"

Joshua Mambwe – Malawi

8. "Zimbabwe matters the most to Africa. Remember Mugabe used to send his army to other other African countries in order to free Africa from the West. I even support Mugabe for quitting the Commonwealth, what did the ordinary black Zimbabwean gain from being a member of the Commonwealth. If you Western people come to Africa you expect us to treat you like kings but when we come to your country you treat us like a piece of trash. I am proud of being a Zimbabwean and I will always be a Zimbabwean."

Samaita – United Kingdom

9. "Zimbabwe has set the example, Africa should follow, quit the Commonwealth! Zimbabwe's destiny is Africa's destiny.

Madimula – Zimbabwe

10. "Congratulations President Mugabe for kicking out Commonwealth from you [your] country. I hope other African leaders follow your example. You are my African Hero. Do not be intimidated by the few stooges who come in the name of opposition [opposition]. I have been to your country four times since indepedence [independence] and I know how good you are."

Abraham W. Selassie – USA

11. "Having lived outside Zimbabwe for some time and then come back, I have come to realise that Western media views are driven more by hatred

for Mugabe than a real understanding of the situation on the ground in Zimbabwe. Sadly those are the same distorted views used by most white countries to arrive at their hardline stances on Zimbabwe. The truth is Zimbabwe is becoming a source of pride for Africa's masses because she is making a stand against the old imperialists in their eyes. Only somebody who is totally ignorant about Africa and Zimbabwe will ask a simpleton's question like 'Does Zimbabwe matter to Africa?'"

Jupiter Punungwe – Zimbabwe

12. "I am sure now everyone realizes that the once Great Zimbabwe matters to Africa more than Australia, Canada and the British government thought. African history is like no other continents on earth. Ours is a history of brotherhood, one of shared struggle against slavery and oppression given to us by the very same colonialists. If Britain, Australia and the US once supported apartheid in South Africa why should any African country think that they are immune to the same brush Zimbabwe; has been painted with."

Eddie Manolo – Zimbabwean in Canada

13. "There is nothing common about the Commonwealth. Mugabe is right to keep white farmers off the Zimbabwean land. Mugabe is fearless and time has come now for Africa to speak with one voice. Commonwealth talks of human rights. That is nonsense. Ironically Nigeria the host, is itself a prominent human rights violator. What kind of human rights lesson can you learn from Jamaica? What has Australia to tell when aborigines who are living like pigs. Mozambique cannot say anything because it's Mugabe who brought them into the Commonwealth. VIVA MUGABE!"

Bruce – Netherlands/New Zealand

14. "At first it was slavery then colonisation and now it's imperialism. The reason for Mugabe to be treated like this is because the international community especially the West knows if every African country follows Mugabe's way Africa will be self sufficent [sufficient]. The West wants Africa to remain poor so that they can manipulate her. We are living like the story of the animal farm if not worse than that."

Brian Chatunga – UK

15. "Imagine what is hapening [happening] in Sudan, DRC, Afghanstan [Afghanistan], Northern Ireland, Israel/Palestine and many other troubled spots. I would like to know whether the Zimbwean [Zimbabwean] situation is as bad as being portrayed by these fortune hunters? (Britain, Australia and New Zealand). The answer is a big No."

Leonard Nkani – Zimbabwe

16. "Africa is not complete without Zimbabwe. If the Africans allow themselves to be divided again, then imperialism is on its way back".

Joey – Canada

17. "Can you ask the same question in regard to other continents? For example: Does Britain matter to Europe?"

Arguer Deng – Australia

18. "The question of Zimbabwe is truly crucial. The West has a narrow outlook on the issue. It is interpreting the whole question purely on their own interests. Mugabe is not the only offender in rigging. Why nothing is said about Eyadema of Togo, Obasanjo of Nigeria, Omar Bongo of Gabon, The Kings and Sultans of Africa and Arabia, and last but not least. Bush of America?"

Msanga Kishashi – Tanzania

19. "Just leave the Africans to deal with Mugabe and no outside interference PLEASE."

Mmuluki – Australia / Botswana

20. "Mugabe is the best and most brave African leader at least he has tried his best to give the resources of this land to their rightful owners. If the white Commonwealth really cared about the black mans' plight why did they not take such a step against Rhodesia or Apartheid South Africa.

Applauled African child of the soil".

21. "I recall a few years back President Mugabe was the brains and driving force of the whole SADC. His actions then and now are just the example of a leader. I think any other president in Africa who is not doing

what Mugabe is doing should just get out of politics because Africa has not tested freedom. Many African leaders are there only to impress the Developed counties."

Samuel Chigaba. – Zimbabwe

22. "I think African countries that are backing Mugabe know what they are doing. African leaders know that Mugabe's decision to redistribute land is the right thing to do. And they understand that Mugabe's isolation from the Commonwealth is not due to frauds and deceptions in elections or human rights violations. If it was so then lots of other countries in Africa will be out of Commonwealth. Let Britain get her hands off Zimbabwe."

Dennis Mwaipola – Tanzania

23. "Zimbabwe sets a good example to the rest of Africa: It has the spine to stand up to the imperialists!"

Mwana Wevhu – Zimbabwe

24. "As much as I do not support Mugabe's dictatorship and violation of human rights, I do not support the isolation of Zimbabwe. I have two sons and I used to punish them whenever they do something wrong. The more I punished them the harder they became until I realised the importance of dialogue. I believe the same thing is happening to Mugabe. The more he becomes isolated and restrictions imposed on him the harder he becomes. But who suffers? Zimbabweans."

Esther – Kenya

25. "Zimbabwe does matter. As long as the international press continues to focus on white farmers you will continue to strengthen Mugabe's position in Africa".

Kaima – Zimbabwean in UK

26. "Zimbabwe does matter to Africa. Until recently, it has been a progressive country, but with the white issue, it is being punished for trying to correct the historical injustices that have been inflicted on not only Zimbabwe but all countries where the whites colonised and are still doing so. I'm strongly in support of my man Mugabe.

LONG LIVE MUGABE."

Seka Taha – Uganda

27. "Indeed Zimbabwe's politics has a great impact not only on African but world politics at large. We should remember that whilst most African countries have gained political independence they have not got the chance to claim their economic independence and the path Zimbabwe has taken might have a bearing on future trends in African politics as people will reclaim what they lost during the colonial years. The only way Africa can deal with the Zimbabwean situation is to critically look at the causative issues of the current situation and find an amicable solution and that can not be achieved without the involvement of the colonial master. Great Britain."

Natahn – UK

28. "Zimbabwe matters. Two [is] issues are mixed up here. One, election fraud. Two, land issues. Mugabe is wrong about the first, so are many other African leaders who are in power by the same means. Mugabe will find support from such "colleagues". On the second issue, Mugabe is right and Britain is on the other side. Why should a minority continue to retain such vast amounts of land which they had acquired wrongly in the past."

Andrew Okello – Iraq (Sulaimaniyah, Kurdistan Iraq)

29. "It is even stupid to ask such a question. Africa is made of many countries, one of them is Zimbabwe so it matters a lot. People should not use the suffering of the Zimbabwean masses to advance their racist remarks. It seems everybody has forgotten that the main issue in Zimbabwe is the land which was first stolen by whites. The hunger or suffering being experienced now is a result of resistance by the racist white countries in the world. They should not hide behind democracy. The truth is they are not worried about my grandmother in Chipinge dying of hunger but are worried by the loss of land suffered by their kith and kin."

Tatenda – South Africa

30. "Zimbabwe is one of Africa's greatest nations and has a brave leadership, both in the ruling party and the opposition. There is no Africa without

Zimbabwe so it's not debatable that it matters significantly to Africa. The only problem seems to be that there is too much outside interference in Zimbabwe's affairs especially from London and Washington. Africa should learn from the Zimbabwe experience that not all from the West is good and colonialism did not die with independence."

Johnson – Kenya

31. "Once land reforms start benefitting [benefiting] the ordinary Zimbabwean citizen, Africa and its people will be taken by storm with land reforms becoming a common policy for Africa. A lot of people do not understand the land hunger in Africa. A lot of African citizens remain poor because they do not have the resources to compete in a free market economy."

Wilberforce Majaji – Zimbabwe, USA

32. "Whatever Mugabe's faults, his policy framework is a testcase. It is interesting that everyone bangs on about the mismanagement and lack of democracy in Zim. These problems are rampant if not endemic in most of Africa, including some countries which are present at CHOGM. It is interesting that Great Britain took centuries to develop parliamentary democracy yet they are expecting countries which are less than 25 years old to operate within a perfect democratic model. Actions and comments by the Zambian and Malawian leaders should be applauded because silence from African leaders will simply lead to modern day slavery and 21st century colonialism through western mechanisms such as the World

Bank, the IMF and WTO. Africa should stand against violence and corruption but should not be coerced into neglecting the brotherhood and solidarity that characterised our collective and ongoing fight for freedom and unity."

Zvirimudendere – UK

34. "I must say that the interest which the Commonwealth has taken in Zimbabwe is not primarily because the Commonwealth is interested in the life of the people in Zimbabwe, but because the interest of white people in Zimbabwe is at stake. When Cameroon was admitted into the Commonwealth it was going through the same political upheaval that Zimbabwe is going through today. But Cameroon was admitted in hope that the Commonwealth would help salvage the situation, but to this

date, nothing much has changed. I detest Mugabe's politics but I am very disappointed by the selective interest of the commonwealth."

David Tonghou – Cameroon-USA

35. "Of course Zimbabwe matters to Africans, every country in Africa matters to Africans. Zimbabwe is not demonised by the West because of governance and democracy, the predicament facing Zimbabwe now arose after Mugabe stood up for black Zimbabweans."

Saied – Canada/Somalia

Appendix 4

My letter to Michael Ancram MP and letters from Andrew George MP, Peter Bottomley MP, Andrew Hopkinson and Anne McIntosh LL.B MP

Appendix 4

The following are my letter to Michael Ancram and letters from Andrew George MP, Peter Bottomley, Andrew Hopkinson and Anne McIntosh LL.B MP. In this appendix, China is referred in the letters from MPs because in my letters to many British politicians I raised the question why Chinese President was welcomed to Britain while he has been regarded by Westminster as a dictator as many others, including President Mugabe.

8 Brindley House
Alfred Road
London W2 5EY

An open letter

The Rt Hon Michael Ancran [Ancram],
QC MP and Conservative Shadow Foreign Secretary
House of Commons
London SW1AOAA

September 23, 2004

Dear Rit Hon Ancran [Ancram],

Thank you for your replying letter of September 07, 2004. I am not surprised at all that you cannot recall whether you have received or not my five page-long letter addressed to you last March. However, I enclose a copy of the same.

I have noted that you have deliberately avoided to answer the crucial points in my recent open letter addressed to you on August 30, 2004. Your recent letter still suggests that when you were in Zimbabwe, and when white farmers had a total control of more than 75% of arable land in Zimbabwe, there was enough food to feed Zimbabweans and much of the African continent. You have not referred to the British tactical economic sanctions on Zimbabwe, which only affect millions of ordinary Zimbabweans, whose you have been expecting to turn against ZANU-FP and President Robert Mugabe. You are still manifesting the persisting and noticeable British neo-colonial propaganda against Mugabe, as he has since introduced a land redistribution programme in Zimbabwe. You still insist on old claims of murder and violence perpetrated by ZANU-PF members, which so far you have not been able to submit the case to the United Nations as a sole mandated international organisation to verily, investigate and take any appropriate action according to its Charter, as it has been doing with the current catastrophic situation in Sudan.

I have to emphasize to you that I do not dare to rule out human rights concerns in Africa, particularly in Zimbabwe. I am conscious of recognising that there are many pressing problems in Africa, poverty starvation, diseases, corruption, economic mismanagement, crisis of democracy, abuse of power, etc, and of course, human rights abuses, which must be addressed without delay. Furthermore, wherever, whether it is committed by white or black or anyone else against whoever, murder is murder torture is torture, violence is violence, etc- and where there is substantial evidence of any act of human rights abuse, it must be condemned publicly. But it becomes very obscure when we see some British politicians like yourself being only interested about the rule of law in Zimbabwe and condemning Robert Mugabe even for simple intimidations of opposition by ZANU-PF supporters at the grassroots, while they themselves turn blind eye to their historical ally George Bush's ignorance of international rule of law and locking up of suspected terrorists in the appalling human conditions at Guantanamo Bay for more than two years without any charge.

In addition, it is also obscure that you seem to be more concerned with murder and violence in Zimbabwe, while your country alongside with the US have been murdering so many innocent Iraqi people, especially Iraqi children under pretext of a safer world community, which has been perceived to be the US, the UK, Israel, Canada- Australia and New Zealand.

You should be reminded that just very recently, the United Nations Secretary General, Koffi Annan [Anan] has made it very clear to the international community which the US and the UK peculiarly champion to protect that Iraq war was illegal and breached UN Charter. Therefore, what you have got left to tell the ignorant international community is that Saddam Hussein was a brutal dictator and that the US and the UK have removed him from power, no matter the loss of lives of many thousands innocent Iraqi people.

When the world saw the appalling images of Abu Ghraib prison in Iraq, saw crimes committed by western civilised and humanitarian soldiers, the political language heard from Westminster was that 'we regret for what happened at Abu Ghraib prison in Iraq, and those responsible for human rights of Iraqi prisoners should be brought to justice But we have to move on'. But we cannot move on from what happened during the 2002 Zimbabwe Presidential election!

While irregularities was a Westminster suitable language to characterize the 2000 US Presidential election, fraud was used as a political language in Westminster to characterize the 2002 Presidential election in Zimbabwe.

Now, I do understand that despite of being unable to explain to the British people me the root causes of the current social and economic problems in Zimbabwe, you as Tony Blair's best devised new approach to fulfil the ambition of a British systematic economic control of Zimbabwe, is through 'regime change' in that sovereign African state. Therefore, since January this year, I have been writing to a selection of British officials, including the Prime Minister- and among several questions, I did set the following question that none of them has been yet able to answer:

The South African President Thabo Mbeki has been blaming Britain and western powers for causing the current crisis in Zimbabwe, thus, for many occasions, he insistently stated publicly that "Britain and other western countries had broken promises, dating from 1979, to fund peaceful land redistribution in Zimbabwe". Now, is Thabo MbekFs statement a fabrication? Is he a liar? Who is right?

I think that the above question should be the starting point before we can talk of food shortage or illegal land grabbing in Zimbabwe. However, I strongly do believe that since all British officials I wrote to have deliberately avoided to answer the above question, you would not be able to come with a clear and fair answer to the same question, rather than expressing concerns with food, free and fair elections, etc, in Zimbabwe. I am looking forward to see that you and the British Government tell the British people who exactly is inviting Britain to intervene or change regime in Zimbabwe. However, certainly, Zimbabwean people have not invited Britain to interfere in their internal affairs; SADC has not requested British military intervention in their sister and sovereign Zimbabwe; AU has not requested it either as it best understands the underlying causes of the current crisis in Zimbabwe, and devotes much efforts in the direction of a peaceful solution, which is hoped to result to a reconciliation of all Zimbabweans, Whereas, whatever happens in Zimbabwe, it is a Zimbabwean and African matter in first place.

Again: *"I believe that, left to ourselves, we can achieve unity on the African continent."* (Julius Nyerere)

Finally, I propose that we meet face to face and discuss this matter in furtherance.

Yours sincerely

Zimi Roberto

ANDREW GEORGE MP
Liberal Democrat Shadow International Development Secretary

HOUSE OF COMMONS
LONDON SW1A OAA

Zimi Roberto   9th December 2005
8 Brindley House
Alfred Road
London W2 5EY   Please Quote Ref: 05/23.1/ag/ew

Dear Zimi Roberto,

RE: CHINESE PRESIDENT'S VISIT TO UK

Thank you for your letter dated 8th November 2005 and for your comments regarding the state visit of China's President to Britain. I do apologise for my delay in replying.

It appears that your letter will have been circulated more widely and I suspect that this will have included my Parliamentary colleague, the Liberal Democrat Shadow Foreign Secretary – Rt. Hon Sir Menzies Campbell MP – who will have appreciated your comments on this matter.

With every good wish.

Yours sincerely,

cc: Rt. Hon Sir Menzies Campbell MP

Peter Bottomley MP
Member of Parliament for Worthing West
House of Commons, London SW1A OAA
Tel: 0207 219 5060 **Fax:** 0207 219 1212
bottomleyp@parliament.uk
Political Secretary: Jo Gardner
gardnerj @parliament.uk

Zimi Roberto
8 Brindley House
Alfred Road
London
W25EY

10ᵗʰ November 2005

PB/BC

Thank you for your letter of 8th November regarding human rights in China and Hu Jintao's visit to London.

I share many of your concerns about democracy and human rights. As a Member of Parliament, it would be inappropriate for me to directly participate in any protests that take place. I did, however, sign Early Day Motion (EDM) 834 on 24ᵗʰ October, which called for the police to facilitate peaceful protests against human rights abuses and ensure that Hu Jintao is not prevented from seeing any protests. On the 27ᵗʰ October, I signed Liam Fox's EDM 883, condemning Chinese infringements on human rights in Tibet. In July, EDM 630 drew attention to the fact that rapid economic change in China has not been matched by political or social reform and called on the British government to press their Chinese counterparts to practice greater tolerance of religious organisations.

I will continue to monitor the situation in China closely, and take appropriate action wherever possible.

Thank you for writing.

Peter Bottomley MP

EDMPrint

Printable Early Day Motion

EDM 834

PEACEFUL PROTESTS DURING THE STATE VISIT OF
PRESIDENT OF CHINA   24.10.2005

40 signatures

Mackinlay, Andrew

Bottomley, Peter
Caton, Martin
Corbyn, Jeremy
Flynn, Paul
Hands, Greg
Holmes, Paul
Law, Peter
Marris, Rob
McDonnell, John
Robertson, Angus
Salmond, Alex
Singh, Marsha
Vis, Rudi
40 signatures
Breed, Colin
Clapham, Michael
Cryer, Ann
Goodman, Helen
Hemming, John
Horwood, Martin
Llwyd, Elfyn
McCafferty, Chris
Penning, Mike
Robinson, Iris
Simpson, Alan
Spink, Bob
Weir, Mike
Campbell, Gregory
Cohen, Harry

Drew, David
Hancock, Mike
Hoey, Kate
Khabra, Piara S
Loughton, Tim
McCrea, Dr William
Price, Adam
Rogerson, Daniel
Simpson, David
Stuart, Graham
Wishart, Pete

That this House calls for an early and detailed statement as to the police operational decisions being made to facilitate peaceful protest against human rights abuses within China during the planned state visit of the President of China and an assurance that the President will not be screened, literally or metaphorically, from such protests simply because it would be uncomfortable for him and embarrassing for the Foreign Office.

http://edmi.parliament.uk/EDMi/EDMDetails.aspx?EDMID=29157&-SESSION=875 01/11/2005

EDMPrint

Printable Early Day Motion

EDM 883

SITUATION IN TIBET   27.10.2005

Fox, Liam   67 signatures

Baker, Norman
Brazier, Julian
Caton, Martin
Drew, David
Fabricant, Michael
Gamier, Edward
Gray, James
Hancock, Mike
Hemming, John
Hoyle, Lindsay
Lepper, David
MacKay, Andrew
McCrea, Dr William
Mercer, Patrick
Mundell, David
Price, Adam
Rogerson, Daniel
Simpson, Alan
Singh, Marsha
Stringer, Graham
Weir, Mike
Winterton, Nicholas
Bottomley, Peter
Breed, Colin
Conway, Derek
Duddridge, James
Farron, Timothy
Gillan, Cheryl
Greenway, John

Hands, Greg
Holloway, Adam
Jenkins, Brian
Lewis, Julian
Mackinlay, Andrew
McDonnell, John
Milton, Anne
Penning, Mike
Randall, John
Salmond, Alex
Simpson, David
Spelman, Caroline
Vis, Rudi
Williams, Roger
Wishart, Pete
Brady, Graham
Campbell, Gregory
Dodds, Nigel
Evans, Nigel
Fraser, Christopher
Goodman, Paul
Hammond, Stephen
Heald, Oliver
Holmes, Paul
Key, Robert
Luff, Peter
MacNeil, Angus
McIntosh, Anne
Moss, Malcolm
Pickles, Eric
Robertson, Angus
Selous, Andrew
Simpson, Keith
Spink, Bob
Wallace, Ben
Winterton, Ann
Wyatt, Derek

That this House regards the destruction of historic buildings, arbitrary security measures and environmental damage in Tibet as infringements upon basic human rights; regrets the British Government's decision not to pursue this, and other human rights issues in China, through the United Nations; and calls on the Prime Minister to raise these issues during the forthcoming visit by President Hu.

http://edmi.parliament.uk/EDMi/EDMDetails.aspx?EDMID=29211&SES-SION=87510/11/2005

EDMPrint

Printable Early Day Motion

EDM 630

CHINA AND RELIGIOUS FREEDOM   19.07.2005

Hoyle, Lindsay   42 signatures

Barrett, John
Brake, Tom
Campbell, Gregory
Crausby, David
Dodds, Nigel
Etherington, Bill
Hancock, Mike
Johnson, Diana R
O'Hara, Edward
Robertson, Angus
Salmond, Alex
Stunell, Andrew
Weir, Mike
Winterton, Nicholas
Battle, John
Breed, Colin
Caton, Martin
Cryer, Ann
Drew, David
Flello, Robert
Hermon, Sylvia
Jones,Lynne
Owen, Albert
Robinson, Iris
Simpson, Alan
Taylor, David
Williams, Betty
Wishart, Pete
Bottomley, Peter
Bryant, Chris

Crabb, Stephen
Dobbin, Jim
Durkan, Mark
George, Andrew
Jenkins, Brian
Lazarowicz, Mark
Pope, Greg
Rosindell, Andrew
Spink, Bob
Vis, Rudi
Wilson, Sammy

That this House condemns the Chinese government for its treatment of religious organisations within the People's Republic of China; notes that the rate of economic change in China has not been matched by political or social reform, with the Communist Party, the world's biggest political party, retaining its monopoly on power and maintaining strict control over the people, cracking down on any signs of opposition and sending outspoken dissidents to labour camps; further notes that this intolerance extends to religious organisations and believers; and therefore calls upon the Government to make representations to the Chinese government to put into practice the principles of tolerance, fairness and peace towards Christians living in China who wish to practise their faith.

http://edmi.parliament.uk/EDMi/EDMDetails.aspx?EDMID=28880&-SESSION=875

01/11/2005

Miss Anne Mclntosh LL.B MP
Member of Parliament for the Vale of York - Tel: 01X45 523S35 or 020
7219 3541 (House of Commons)
HOUSE OF COMMONS
LONDON SW1A 0AA

Mr Zimi Roberto
8 Brindley House
Alfred Road
London
W25EY

16 November 2005

Dear Mr Roberto

Thank you for your letter, dated 8 November, regarding the visit to Britain of
Chinese President Hu Jintoa.

As you will be aware, China has been a one-party state since Mao Zedong
won the Chinese civil war in 1949. Although it remains Communist in name,
Deng Xiaoping (who succeeded Mao) began introducing a market economy
in the early 1980s. His successors have taken those policies further, allowing
markets to develop in industrial as well as agricultural sectors. Most of China's
economic growth occurs in various 'Special Economic Zones' — largely in
big cities on the coast — where there is almost no state interference in the
economy.

Economic liberalisation has certainly not been accompanied by any extension
of political freedom. Although China has refrained from high-profile massacres since Tiananmen Square in 1989, political dissent is still suppressed.
China's rulers are so paranoid about the existence of independent sources of
authority that they clamp down on innocuous, but large and independent,
religious organisations such as the Falun Gong.

The Government has repeatedly failed to condemn such abuses, despite promising to make it a central facet of their foreign policy. Indeed, in its human
rights report the Foreign Office described the 'forced eviction of hundreds
of thousands of home owners throughout China' and the seizure of 'farming
land' for development. When Zimbabwe did the same, the Prime Minister
said 'what is happening in Zimbabwe is a disgrace.' I certainly agree that the

actions of President Mugabe are disgraceful, but am concerned that the Prime Minister has failed to condemn such abuses in China.

This disparity is a key question that the Government must address.

However, whilst China still has a number of important issues to address, President Hu Jintoa has expressed a willingness to look at these concerns, and his visit to the UK has given British parliamentarians on all sides the chance to raise such matters with him. I can assure you, for example, that Michael Howard utilised the opportunity to vehemently express concern over human rights abuses taking place in China at his meeting with the President. As China modernises economically, such international pressure will be crucial to ensure that social freedoms are advanced and improved.

This situation is clearly different to that of President Mugabe in Zimbabwe. Over the past few years the political, humanitarian and economic situation in Zimbabwe has worsened: over half the population face food shortages; hospitals have been closed; some water supplies have been turned off; inflation is soaring; and human rights abuses continue on a daily basis.

Zimbabwe needs to be confronted head-on. The EU must impose tougher sanctions against Zimbabwe and mast also widen them to freeze the assets of those who bankroll Mugabe. The EU has missed an opportunity to exert pressure on the Mugabe regime. The British Government should take Zimbabwe to the UN Security Council. It should propose a resolution to send UN observers to Zimbabwe and monitor food distribution. It is now essential that Zimbabwe's neighbours, led by South Africa, take action to ensure that Zimbabwe does not spiral further into disaster. Real pressure must be applied and if they refuse to act, then the international community will need to examine further options available to it.

I hope that you will recognise that in such circumstances, President Mugabe is unlikely to be swayed by meeting British parliamentarians, and indeed, in previous circumstances has used such opportunities to present himself as an international statesman. Until he begins to act in such a manner, notably by respecting human rights and restoring the rule of law, can he expect to welcomed back into the wider international community.

Thank you, once again, for taking the time to raise this important matter with me.

Yours sincerely

Miss Anne McIntosh LLB MP
Member of Parliament for the Vale of York
Shadow Minister for Foreign Affairs

Foreign &
Commonwealth
Office

Africa Department
(Southern)
King Charles Street
London
SW1A 2AL

Tel: 0207 008 4263
Fax: 0207 008 3940
E-mail: Andrew.
Hopkinson@fco.gov.uk

02 February 2004

Zimi Roberto
8 Brindley House
Alfred Road
London
W25EY

ZIMBABWE

Thank you for your letter of 19 January to Chris Mullin, Minister for Africa.
I have been asked to reply.

You raised a number of questions about the UK government's policies towards Zimbabwe.

You say that no African leader publicly criticised Mugabe at the
Commonwealth Heads of Government meeting in Abuja in December 2003.
But at Abuja Commonwealth leaders agreed, by consensus, to continue in-
definitely Zimbabwe's suspension from the Councils of the Commonwealth.
Considering the consistent and widespread abuse of human rights in
Zimbabwe continued suspension was the only acceptable outcome.

Following this decision the Government of Zimbabwe withdrew Zimbabwe
from the

Commonwealth. This will do nothing to ease the crisis in Zimbabwe and will only increase further the country's isolation from the international community. The ties of affection between the Commonwealth and the people of Zimbabwe remain and we look forward to a time when a democratic Zimbabwe that respects the Harare Principles can be welcomed back into the organisation.

You mention President Mbeki's claim that the situation in Zimbabwe has been caused by the UK and Western powers. The current crisis in Zimbabwe is due to ZANU (PF)'s disastrous policies which have led to inflation of almost 600 per cent and unemployment of over 70%.

In addition, it is estimated that six million people (over half the population) will need food aid during the January to April pre-harvest period. Rather than being the cause of the crisis, the UK is helping the people of Zimbabwe. Since September 2001 we have provided £62 million in aid; £20 million in the current financial year alone. Over the coming months we will be providing further humanitarian aid. Hardly the actions of a government which merely wishes to protect its white settler, colonial kith and kin.

Nor is it the case that Britain and the other western countries have broken their promises to fund peaceful land redistribution. We have consistently said that we would support a land reform programme that was transparent, fair and legal and that was carried out within a macro-economic framework that formed part of a wider Zimbabwe Government programme to reduce poverty. These are the principles agreed by donors and the Government of Zimbabwe at the Land Conference in 1998. The Government of Zimbabwe's "fast track" land reform programme is not consistent with any of these principles. At the Lancaster House conference the then Foreign Secretary, Lord Carrington said that the UK would be prepared to provided technical assistance for re-settlement schemes and capital aid for agricultural development projects and infrastructure. He went to say that the costs would be very substantial and well beyond the capacity of any individual donor country. There was no sum of money mentioned, no fund established, and the UK made it clear that it could not be the only donor to any land reform programme.

In the 1980's Britain donated £47 million towards land reform in Zimbabwe. £3.3 million was eventually returned by the Government of Zimbabwe unspent.

The EU has imposed targeted measures against Mugabe and 78 leading

ZANU (PF) members, including a travel ban and asset freeze. They do not include economic sanctions, or any other measures which would harm the ordinary Zimbabwean people. These are due for renewal later this month and we will be looking with our EU colleagues at ways of strengthening them and making them more effective whilst continuing to avoid any action which would add to the sufferings of the ordinary Zimbabwean people.

Finally you mention Mugabe's knighthood. We are keeping this under review. However, our current priorities are to relieve the sufferings of the Zimbabwe people and to work with our international partners to bring about the return of democratic governance which respects human rights and the rule of law.

Andrew Hopkinson
Africa Department (Southern)
cc:

Miss Anne McIntosh LL.B MP
Member of Parliament for the Vale of York - Tel: OIS45 523X35 or 020 72
I1) 3541 (House of Commons)

HOUSE OF COMMON LONDON SW1A OAA

Mr Zimi Roberto
8 Brindley House
Alfred Road
London
W25EY

5 September 2005

Dear Mr Roberto

Thank you very much for your letter, dated 5 July, regarding land reform in Zimbabwe. I must apologise for the delay in responding to you, which has been unavoidably caused by the summer recess.

In your letter you ask whether the following statement by the South African President, Thabo Mbeki, is true:

"Britain and other western countries had broken promises, dating from 1979, to fund peaceful land redistribution in Zimbabwe…"

I therefore would like to take this opportunity to explain in some detail the background to the situation and show that it is in fact the Zimbabwe Government that has broken its commitment on this matter.

At the time of Zimbabwe's Independence in 1980, the best agricultural land was owned mainly by large, commercial farms, often of more than 1,000 hectares each.

Poor families were crowded into the less productive communal areas, on land holdings that were often less than one hectare.

The British Government believes that land reform is central to Zimbabwe's development. Britain has been a strong advocate of effective and well-managed land reform in Zimbabwe since Independence. A more equitable distribution of land is essential to reduce poverty and to contribute to the country's long-term economic and social future. But to be effective, the British Government believes that such reform must be carried out within the rule of law; be transparent and fair; and within a well- managed economic policy framework that contributes both to poverty reduction and Zimbabwe's economic prosperity.

The negotiations which led to the Lancaster House Agreement brought Independence to Rhodesia following Ian Smith's illegal Unilateral Declaration of Independence in 1965, and was signed in December 1979. The parties represented during the conference were: the British Government, the Zimbabwe-Rhodesia Administration and the Patriotic Front led by Robert Mugabe and Joshua Nkomo.

At the Lancaster House talks, the UK agreed to contribute to the costs of land reform and to rally the support of the international donor community. The UK's position was set out by Lord Carrington, the Conference Chairman, in a statement made to the plenary session on 11 October 1979. He said:

"We recognise that the future Government of Zimbabwe, whatever its political complexion, will wish to extend land ownership. The Government can of course purchase land for agricultural settlement, as we all have seen. The Independence Constitution will make it possible to acquire under-utilised land compulsorily, provided that adequate compensation is paid.

Any resettlement scheme would clearly have to be carefully prepared and implemented to avoid adverse effects on production.

The Zimbabwe Government might well wish to draw in outside donors such as the World Bank in preparing and implementing a full-scale agricultural development plan.

The British Government recognise the importance of this issue to a future Zimbabwe Government and will be prepared, within the limits imposed by our financial resources, to help. We should for instance be ready to provide technical assistance for settlement schemes and capital aid for agricultural development projects and infrastructure. If an agricultural development bank or some equivalent institution were set up to promote agricultural development including land settlement schemes, we would be prepared to contribute to the initial capital.

The costs would be very substantial indeed, well beyond the capacity, in our judgement of any individual donor country, and the British Government cannot 'commit itself at this stage to a specific share in them. We should however be ready to support the efforts of the government of independent Zimbabwe to obtain inter-

national assistance for these purposes. "

There was therefore no provision in the Lancaster House Agreement to establish a specific fund to support land reform. However, as promised at Lancaster House, the British Government did play a full part both before and after the international Zimbabwe Donors' Conference (ZIMCORD) of March 1981 to encourage Western donors to take part and to respond generously to Zimbabwe's requirements. ZIMCORD succeeded in raising $Z 70m (£17m) for development in Zimbabwe, including land reform. The Constitution of Zimbabwe agreed at Lancaster House entrenched protection for property rights for the first ten years of Independence. The Government's acquisition of land was limited to the willing buyer/willing seller principle. Thereafter, the Zimbabwe Parliament would be able to alter the Constitution in accordance with its own legislation.

Between 1980 and 1985, the UK provided £47m for land reform: £20m as a specific Land Resettlement Grant and £27m in the form of budgetary support to help meet the Zimbabwe Government's own contribution to the programme. The Land Resettlement Grant was signed in 1981, and substantially spent by 1988.

An evaluation of land resettlement in 1988 by the then UK Overseas Development Administration (ODA) showed that real progress had been made. The report suggested measures for further improving the UK-funded programme. The 1988 report was sent to the Zimbabwe Government, but ODA received no response.

The UK Land Resettlement Grant finally closed in 1996 with £3m still unspent. The UK Government sought proposals from the Zimbabwe Government on spending the remaining balance. A further technical mission by the ODA in 1996 resulted in new proposals for UK support for land reform. The Zimbabwe Government responded towards the end of 1996, but no agreement was reached before the UK General Election in May 1997.

In September 1998, with UK encouragement, the Zimbabwe Government hosted a Land Conference in Harare, involving all major international donors and the multilateral institutions. Issues raised in the ODA's 1996 report were considered at the Conference. The UK participated constructively and endorsed the basic principles for land reform agreed at the Conference, as did the Zimbabwe Government. Those principles included the need for: transparency, respect for the rule of law, poverty reduction, affordability and consistency with Zimbabwe's wider economic interests.

The 1998 Conference agreed a two-year Inception Phase, during which Government resettlement schemes would be tried alongside ideas from the private sector and civil society. In May 1999, consultants began work to identify ways in which the UK Government could provide further support for land reform in Zimbabwe. Terms of reference for a follow-up visit were agreed with the Zimbabwe Government in September 1999. Work on UK support for land reform in Zimbabwe was interrupted by the illegal farm occupations and the subsequent violence in the run-up to the 2000 Parliamentary elections.

I can assure you, Britain remains willing to support a land reform programme that is carried out in accordance with the principles agreed by donors and the Zimbabwe Government in 1998. This is also the position of the broad donor community. We are not imposing any new conditions.

In the absence of a Government-led programme which Britain felt able to support, the Department for International Development (DFID, ODA's successor) established in March 2000 a £5m Land Resettlement Challenge Fund to support private sector and civil society-led resettlement initiatives. Unfortunately, the Zimbabwe Government has not allowed such private sector initiatives to proceed. It has instead pressed ahead with its Fast Track Resettlement Programme, which the international community has been unable to support.

In late 2000, the UNDP Administrator proposed to the Zimbabwe Government a slowing down of its fast track resettlement programme to fit Zimbabwe's implementation capacity; independent monitoring of the situation in commercial farming areas; the promotion of internal dialogue; and the possible resumption of UNDP technical assistance. UNDP stressed the importance of a transparent, just and fair land reform that respects the rule of law and in accordance with the principles agreed at the 1998 Land Conference and laws of Zimbabwe. The Government's reply suggested that it was not willing to move on the major issues blocking re-engagement by the international community.

A group of Commonwealth Foreign Ministers (including the United Kingdom and Zimbabwe) met in Abuja on 6 September 2001 to discuss Zimbabwe. On land reform, they agreed that reform must be implemented in a fair, just and sustainable manner, in the interest of all the people of Zimbabwe, and that any land reform programme should be on the basis of the UNDP proposals of December 2000. The Government of

Zimbabwe agreed to honour the principles enshrined in the Harare Commonwealth Declaration, to prevent further occupation of farm lands, to restore the rule of law, to take firm action against violence and intimidation and to honour the freedom of expression. At that meeting the UK re-affirmed its commitment to a significant financial contribution to such a land reform programme and gave an undertaking to encourage other international donors to do the same.

In November 2001, the Government of Zimbabwe amended the Land Acquisition Act to allow it to allocate land without giving owners the right to contest the seizures. This contravenes the letter and spirit of Abuja.

Regrettably, the credibility of Abuja has been irreversibly damaged by Zimbabwe's scant regard for its commitments (respect for the rule of law, end to violence and intimidation). The UNDP report of 2002 on land concludes that Zimbabwe's fast track land reform programme is chaotic, unsustainable and lacking transparency.

We deplore the approach adopted to recent land reform which has disrupted commercial and communal farming alike. It has been violent and unfair to farm owners and farm workers, and damaging to agricultural production and the national economy. Up until 2000, commercial agriculture accounted for more than 40% of Zimbabwe's national exports, and was the basis for agro-industry which has since collapsed.

Even the resettled poor will be left in worse circumstances than before for many years. The Zimbabwe Government's strategy has not adhered to the principles for land reform agreed with donors at the 1998 Land Conference in Harare, and neither has it implemented the programme consistently with its own stated policy and criteria, nor with its repeatedly changed laws and regulations.

We believe that land reform carried out for political expediency and without reference to its long term effects will tend to fail because it will not make people better off. Land reform needs to deliver increased prosperity for the many if it is to be credible. Current policies of allocating land through patronage to politically influential groups will not reduce poverty. The genuinely poor, not just particular interest groups must be seen to benefit through a properly planned programme that ensures that basic infrastructure and services are available for the settlers. Transparency means that there must be objective criteria and proper procedures for selecting settlers for all resettlement schemes and means of monitoring and publicising what actually happens.

To date there has been no transparency in the Fast Track programme.

It is also worth remembering that since independence the UK has provided more than £500m in bilateral support for development in Zimbabwe - more than any other donor. In total, the wider donor community has provided over $2bn in assistance. The UK continues to provide annual support for emergency relief and to alleviate HIV/AIDs suffering. The UK has also contributed to development in Zimbabwe through the international financial institutions. The UK funds around 18% of EC spending.

The political, humanitarian and economic situation in Zimbabwe is worsening. Over half the population face food shortages, hospitals have been closed, some water supplies have been turned off, inflation is soaring and human rights abuses continue on a daily basis. The 'quiet diplomacy' approach that this Labour Government has adopted is just rhetoric and is simply not working. It is critical that the international community intervenes.

My Conservative colleagues and I believe that Zimbabwe needs to be confronted head-on. The EU must impose tougher sanctions against Zimbabwe and must also widen them to freeze the assets of those who bankroll Mugabe. The EU has missed an opportunity to exert pressure on the Mugabe regime. The British Government should take Zimbabwe to the UN Security Council. It should propose a resolution to send UN observers to Zimbabwe and monitor food distribution. It is now essential that Zimbabwe's neighbours, led by South Africa, take action to ensure that Zimbabwe does not spiral further into disaster.

Thank you very much, once again, for taking the time to raise this important matter with me.

Yours sincerely

Miss Anne McIntosh LLB MP
Member of Parliament for the Vale of York
Shadow Minister for Foreign Affairs

Glossary

Esoteric: difficult to understand

Unrequited: unanswered

Trotting: pushing, running, jogging

Last troes: a spasm of pain – last pain when you are close to die

Consternation: a feeling of bewilderment and dismay often caused by something unexpected

Bewilderment: to confuse or puzzle somebody

Trepidation: fear or uneasiness about the future or a future event

Plethora: a very large amount or number of something, especially an excessive amount, e.g. excessive of meetings

Repugnant: offensive and completely

Disseminate: to distribute or spread something, especially information, or become widespread

Deferential: showing or expressing polite, respect or courtesy

Memento: an object given or kept as a reminder of or in memory of somebody or something

Perjury: lying under oath, false swearing

Swindler: cheat, trickster, charlatan, fraud, faker

Charlatan: false expert, somebody who falsely claims a special skill or expertise

Arbitrary: random, subjective and uninformed

Abstract: theoretical, conceptual, based on general principles or theories rather than on specific instances

Ideology: a closely organised system of beliefs, values, and other ideas forming the basis of a social, economic, or political philosophy or program – a set of beliefs, values, and opinions that shapes the way an individual or a group such as a social class thinks, acts, and understands the world

Subjugation: the act or process of bringing somebody, especially a people or nation, under the control of another, for example, by military conquest

Subsidy: finance economics a grant or gift of money from a government to a private company, organization, or charity to help it to continue to function

Reminiscence: the recollection of past experiences or events in speech or writing, or the act of recalling the past

Subversive: intended or likely to undermine or overthrow a government or other institution

Rational: governed by, or showing evidence of, clear and sensible thinking and judgment, based on reason rather than emotion or prejudice

Tarnish: to damage somebody's reputation or good name, or to become damaged

Overstep: to go beyond the limit of something; overstep the bounds of your authority

Foster: to provide a child with care and upbringing; to encourage the development of something

Audacious: bold, daring, or fearless, especially in challenging assumptions or conventions; overconfident, risky

Incredulously: unable or unwilling to believe something or completely unconvinced by it

Insidious: slowly and subtly harmful or destructive

Subtly: ingeniously, deviously

Pernicious: causing great harm, destruction, or death

Fledged: transitive verb to provide or cover something with feathers or something similar

Ravish: by force

Innuendo: an indirect remark or gesture that usually carries a suggestion of impropriety

Smear: to deliberately spread damaging rumours about somebody

Sever: to cut through something or cut off, or be cut through or off

Redeem: to make something acceptable or pleasant in spite of its negative qualities or aspects; to restore yourself to favour or to somebody's good opinion

Blatant: so obvious or conspicuous as to be impossible to hide; blatant falsehoods

Audacious: bold, daring, or fearless, especially in challenging assumptions or conventions

Murambatsvina: Zimbabwean local language meaning restore order

Chimurenga: Zimbabwean local language meaning National Uprising

Bibliography

Alec Russell – Big Men – Little People – Encounters in Africa – 1999 – Published by Macmilan Publishers Ltd – London, Basingstoke and Oxford

African Magazine publications.

African residents in the United Kingdom and visitors from Africa, including from Zimbabwe.

Allan G. Johnson – 2001 – Second Edition – The Blackwell Dictionary of Sociology –Published by Blackwell Publishers Ltd – 108 Cowley Road – Oxford OX4 1JF –UK.

Andrew Heywood – Political Theory – Second edition – 1999 – Published by Palgrave – Houndmills, Basingstoke – Hampshire RG21 6XS and Fifth Avenue – New York – N.Y. 10010.

Anti-Apartheid, a history of the movement in Britain – 2005 – Published by 'The Merlin Press Ltd' – London.

Blood and Soil, Land, Politics and Conflict Prevention in Zimbabwe and South Africa – 2004 – Published by International Crisis Group – Brussels.

Bob Woodward – Bush at War – 2002 – Published by Simon & Schuster Rockefeller Center – New York.

David Whynes – Welfare State Economics – Published in 1992

Geoff Hill – The Battle for Zimbabwe – 2003 – Published by Zebra Press – South Africa.

E. J. Hobsbawn – The Age of Empire – 1875-1914 – Published by Abacus in 1994.

Global Witness – A crude awakening – Published by Global Witness Ltd

Joshua S. Goldstein – International Relations – Second Edition – 1996 – Published by HaperCollins – USA.

Georges Nzongola-Ntalaja – The Congo, from Leopold to Kabila – 2002 – Published by Zed Books Ltd – London and New York.

Gino J. Naldi – The Organization of African Unity – An Analysis of its Role – 1989 – Published by Mansell Publishing Ltd – London.

http://news.bbc.co.uk/l/hi/world/africa/3292151.stm 12/01/2004 -

BBCNEWS World Africa Does Zimbabwe matter to Africa?

Ian Budge – Ivor Crewe – David Mackay – Ken Newton – 1998 – The New British Politics – Published by Addison Wesley Longman Limited – Edinburgh – Harlow – Essex CM20 2JE.

James Joll – Europe since 1870 – First published by Weidenfeld & Nicolson in 1973

John L. Seitz – An Introduction – 1997 – Global Issues – Published by Blackwell Publishers Inc – 350 Main Street – Madlen – Massachusetts – 02148 – USA.

Matthew Parris – Great Parliamentary Scandals – 1995 – Published by Robson Books Ltd – London.

Namibia High commission in London-United Kingdom.

Newspapers: Guardian, Independent, Times, Daily Mail, Sun, Evening Standard, Metro.

Stephen J. Lee – European Dictatorships – 1918 – 1945 – Second Edition – 2000 – Published by Methuen & Co Ltd – London.

The Guinness Book of Answers – 9th edition – Guinness published Ltd – 1993.

The Longman Encyclopedia – First Edition – 1989 – Published by Longman Group UK Limited – Longman House – Burnt Mill – Harlow CM20 2JE – England.

The New Encyclopedia Britannica – MICROPÆDIA ready reference – 1994 – 15th Edition – Volume 4 – Printed in the USA

Wayne Ellwood – 2001 - The No-Nonsense Guide to Globalization – Published by New International Publications Ltd – Oxford OX4 1BW – UK.

Zimbabwe High Commission in London-United Kingdom.

Printed in the United States
By Bookmasters

Printed in the United States
By Bookmasters